AFTER EDEN

AFTER EDEN

The Secularization of American Space in
the Fiction of Willa Cather
and Theodore Dreiser

Conrad Eugene Ostwalt, Jr.

Lewisburg
Bucknell University Press
London and Toronto: Associated University Presses

Associated University Presses
440 Forsgate Drive
Cranbury, NJ 08512

Associated University Presses
25 Sicilian Avenue
London WC1A 2QH, England

Associated University Presses
P.O. Box 488, Port Credit
Mississauga, Ontario
Canada L5G 4M2

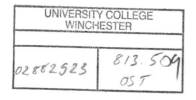
The paper used in this publication meets the requirements of the American National Standard for Permanence of Paper for Printed Library Materials Z39.48-1984.

Library of Congress Cataloging-in-Publication Data

Ostwalt, Conrad Eugene, 1959–
    After Eden : the secularization of American space in the fiction
of Willa Cather and Theodore Dreiser / Conrad Eugene Ostwalt, Jr.
        p.   cm.
    Includes bibliographical references.
    ISBN 0-8387-5168-7 (alk. paper)
    1. American fiction—20th century—History and criticism.
2. Space and time in literature.   Cather, Willa, 1873–1947—
Criticism and interpretation.   4. Dreiser, Theodore, 1871–1945—
Criticism and interpreation.   5. Secularism in literature.
6. Religion and literature.   7. Setting (Literature)   I. Title.
PS374.S7308   1990   89-42505
813'.5209384—dc20   CIP

For Mary,

for adding color to my world

Contents

Acknowledgements

Political rhetoric and religious trends over the past decade and a half have raised significant questions for me about how Americans perceive their own nation. Our nation suffers an identity crisis; we seem to want to envision and embrace an America that no longer exists; we are confused because our paradigmatic, or mythical, America is sacred while we live in a secular land and time. I have tried to unravel some of this confusion in this book, and if for no other reason, I have undertaken this project in order to clarify for myself the relationship between sacred paradigms and secular realities as they interrelate in the American cultural matrix.

The genesis for this study came during my summer reading while I was a graduate student and grew from graduate research to the current product. As a result, it is not surprising that I am deeply indebted to my preceptors and teachers. In particular, Peter Kaufman and Grant Wacker, mentors and friends, have encouraged and influenced my work more than they can know. Also, Stuart Henry, William Poteat, and Kenny Williams provided insightful critique and guidance as this book took shape. Finally, a special thanks goes to Wesley A. Kort, whose support, criticism, encouragement, and "open door" have guided my research and writing for several years.

In addition to my teachers, colleagues and friends at Duke University and at the University of North Carolina at Chapel Hill have been a tremendous help in the completion of this book. In particular, Julia Hardy and Joel Martin were always there when I needed them. Also, the Department of Religion at Lafayette College, especially Stephen E. Lammers, Robert L. Cohn, and Earl A. Pope, provided encouragement and support during revision of this manuscript. And most recently, as the book took its final form, Alan Hauser and my colleagues in the Department of Philosophy-Religion at Appalachian State University have assisted in numerous capacities. Others at Appalachian have provided special assistance toward completing the book in its final stages: Peter Cohen, David Ball, and the folks in "Career Planning and

Placement" and "Student Employment" have helped me maintain my sanity; Rusty Ellis helped with reproductions, letters, and the "nuts and bolts;" Stan Latta and Mark Williams provided able criticism, skillful analysis, and an unbridled willingness to help. Finally, the administration and staff at Bucknell University Press and Associated University Presses have been most helpful and patient during the production of this work.

I acknowledge permission to quote from the following material: "Prairie Spring" and excerpts from *O Pioneers!* by Willa Cather, copyright 1913 and 1941 by Willa Sibert Cather. Reprinted by permission of Houghton Mifflin Company. "Neighbour Rosicky," from *Obscure Destinies* by Willa Cather, copyright 1930, 1932 by Willa Cather, renewed 1958, 1960 by the executors of the estate of Willa Cather. Reprinted by permission of Alfred A. Knopf, Inc.

My greatest debt is to my family. In different ways, my in-laws, my brother and sisters, Angela, Donna, and Mark, and my parents have all contributed to this book. I only hope this work reflects the Truths that only brothers and sisters can provide, and my parents' teaching that "any job worth doing is worth doing right." Finally, I thank my wife, Mary, by dedicating this work to her, for it is truly the product of her effort as much as mine. Through our nine years of marriage, and our five before that, she more than anything has been my link to wholeness.

AFTER EDEN

1

"America" as Paradise Lost

Spatial Disorientation at the End of the Nineteenth Century

Among the changes in American culture during the nineteenth century, none was more important than the transformation of its sense of religious identity and purpose. This transformation affected all areas of life, but its consequences for the American understanding of space were particularly dramatic. The appearance of both the American landscape and cityscape had changed by the end of the nineteenth century as the spatial understanding of America changed from sacred to secular. As this transition of attitude developed, Americans were left stranded by a rapidly advancing world that undermined cherished conceptions about their meaningful and familiar home. America, the agrarian and blessed state, was gone. Nineteenth-century Americans were estranged by this loss, and it took them until the beginning of the next century to make sense of a new spatial orientation toward their world. In other words, the American at the turn of the century was involved in a process that exchanged a beleaguered system of belief and worldview for one more suitable to the altered cultural situation.

The result of this exchange of worldviews—the outcome of this movement from disorientation to orientation—is the secularization of American space. It is a changed and secularized American environment that confronts Americans at the turn of the century, but this secularization also becomes the occasion for the appearance of new beliefs and affirmations concerning spatial orientation and relationships. This chapter explores the exchange of a sacred world for a secular one—an exchange that was religiously significant and culturally crucial for the nineteenth-century American whose identity suffered challenge from an ephemeral environment.

1. The World That was Lost: The American Dream and the Sacred World

The idea of a sacred space emerged and flourished from the beginnings of America and was firmly rooted in the American dream of possibility and opportunity. This dream was articulated by John Winthrop, who set the tone for the new country in his 1630 sermon, "A Modell of Christian Charity." "The Lord will be our God and delight to dwell among us, as his owne people and will commaund a blessing upon us in all our wayes, . . . for wee must Consider that wee shall be as a Citty upon a Hill, the eies of all people are uppon us. . . ."[1] From these words of Winthrop, and from the rhetoric of statesmen and politicians for decades to come, grew a cluster of ideas that granted American public life a certain religious quality. With this "American Civil Religion," there arose a tendency to sacralize societal and cultural values in order to maintain national identity. Consequently, an elaborate structure of religious convictions in America centered on an implied creed concerning America as a promised land and Americans as a chosen people. According to this creed, God granted Americans special sanction, and as long as the country continues to seek the will of God, God will continue to smile upon it. Thus was born the American dream of possibility.

These notions are present in American history in the forms of religious rhetoric, symbolism, and iconography. One sees their force in the way historical events are transformed into myth. For example, Abraham Lincoln's execution on Good Friday elevated him to the status of a Christ figure for popular America. He was the great liberator who sacrificed his life for the salvation of his country—the chosen land and people. Sacvan Bercovitch brilliantly traces some of these symbolic ideas surrounding America's sacred identity in his study of a recurring rhetorical form. This form, the "American Jeremiad," was an American ritual that helped to shape the development of America from its inception as a Puritan community. The American jeremiad was the supreme ritual for the gospel of ambiguity that explained America's curious civil religious ideology. This religious ambiguity originated as the bridge between an eschatological heaven and a this-worldly earth. Thus, the American jeremiad is foundational to the Puritan theocratic ideal and to the subsequent American love affair with manifest destiny and exploitative possibility.[2]

Because of the ambiguous conception of America that Bercovitch describes, the Puritan covenantal relationship with God led
to two concerns. The first concerned America as a sacred world.
For the Puritan, America appeared in terms of God's eternal
promise to the Puritan fathers. These New World founders
viewed the American continent as the symbol of the Puritan mission to establish a theocratic rule and to act as a "City upon a
Hill"—as a beacon shining from the wilderness of the New World
to the darkness of the Old.[3] However, this is tempered by a second
concern for America as the land that serves the master of human
initiative—human opportunity. Not only is the Puritan mission
one for the glory of God, but it is also one to secure freedom from
European oppression for the Puritan social group. Thus, Bercovitch presents a picture of America that is governed on the one
hand by the teleological threat of "apocalyptic disaster" and the
eschatological promise of "millennial disaster" but that receives
impetus, on the other hand, from the human initiative of America's "chosen band."[4] This tension between divine and human initiative, between future and present time, and between sacred and
secular worldviews helps to explain the American conception of
America. This tension is inherent in the vision of an America that
is the benefactor of God and that offers opportunity to all.

Bercovitch goes on to recognize that the dominant symbol of
this ambiguous America, at least in the postrevolutionary period,
was that of America as sacred place.[5] Furthermore, this conception of America reached its height with the romantic tradition in
the early to mid-nineteenth century. The Emersonian world was
one that was teleologically oriented within an Edenic environment.[6] This romantic vision, which is based upon the teleological
standard, involves the transcendence of humankind beyond profane existence to confront and to participate in divine reality or
radical otherness. As a result, for the Emersonian, the sacred
dream of American space informs the description of transcendent
reality as it reveals itself in the American world of natural harmony and human possibility.

This American dream matured as it perpetuated itself most ef-
fectively through the romantic vision and the sacred worldview
that the romantics presupposed. The American myth filtered
through the two cardinal tenets of the Emersonian world and
emerged espousing two poles to the dream of possibility. On the
one hand, the romantic vision views the natural realm in sacred
terms—nature is good and is the receptacle of otherness. On the

other hand, human beings and the social world also participate in the sacred order of the universe. The divine resides in the social as well as in the natural world as human society becomes the occasion for divine presence.

This romantic filter gave the American dream of possibility two poles from which to view its idea of sacred America; natural America was sacred and social America was sacred. Catherine Albanese describes this bipolar conception of America as the "twin hopes" of the American dream as lived out at transcendentalist communities such as Brook Farm. These transcendental social experiments combined both poles of the idea of sacred America as their participants sought to create a perfect utopian society while living in total harmony with nature.[7] However, this bipolar conception of America did not disintegrate with the transcendentalist communities but continued in a dual version of the American dream as the nineteenth century progressed. Not only was the natural world the sacred place of possibility in the form of the West, but the social world was the place of opportunity in the form of cities and urban environments. Thus, the two symbolic places of the American dream of opportunity in the nineteenth century developed from the romantic presupposition of a sacred America. A short examination of this romantic dream highlights the bipolar understanding of sacred America that suffered transformation and redefinition as the century proceeded.

To explore the sacred world that the romantic writers promulgated, one might ask the question that plagued Ishmael—"Why did the old Persians hold the sea holy?," and why was Moby Dick the awful "manifestation of God's power?" The answer lies in Emerson's struggle to locate "the divine *aura* which breathes through forms . . ." and with his assertion that "man has anything in him divine." One finds the answer in Giles Gunn's claim that Melville presupposes an "ever-emergent creator God" who is "immanent in Nature but not identical with it. . . ."[8] The culmination of this struggle comes with the romantic assertion of a sacred world—a world that contains God—a world through which human beings gain access to the transcendent. This sacred world is like Nantucket where "the first dead American whale was stranded."[9] Nantucket is the last point of land before Ishmael begins his fateful journey; it is the last habitat of the known and familiar world before one begins a journey into an unknown and strange environment. As such, Nantucket is the meeting place between the known and the unknown—between security and estrangement—between humanity and God—between thisness and otherness. In short, Nantucket (and the romantic world) is the sacred garden of Eden where God and Adam meet face to face.

Thus, the romantic writers conceive a world with sacred import—a world that lends access to the transcendent as opposed to a secular world that offers no transcending possibilities. But how is this presented in their work? The sacred significance of environment usually appears in relation to the romantic conception of nature. This understanding is ambiguous and views nature as the receptacle of otherness. As a result, the romantic poets approach nature in at least two different ways: they desire communion with nature, yet they seek to transcend it. This ambivalence toward the natural world has fascinated many scholars of the romantic period and has led to fruitful insights concerning the romantic attitude of communion with and transcendence of nature.

In *A World Elsewhere,* Richard Poirier examines the romantic approach to the world as expressed in the transcendentalism of Ralph Waldo Emerson. Poirier isolates "two attitudes toward existent environments . . . in American literature: the one imitative, . . . the other creative. . . ."[10] The creative pole is Poirier's main concern and is best exemplified by Emerson. The Emersonian world construction is creative and visionary, and it arises out of the ability to envision and realize new worlds and new possibilities. Yet, before visionaries can build and transcend to new worlds, they must first experience unity with this world. The best way to do this is to experience some type of unity or communion with nature.[11]

The need to unite with the natural universe derives directly from Emerson's notion that the "other" is contained within and is revealed through nature.[12] This monistic philosophy of life allows Emerson to view creation as inherently good and, thus, worthy of egalitarian unity. Because the universe is infused by Spirit and because it is naturally good, harmony between humanity and nature can only result in a meaningful encounter with alterity—with a meaningful experience of that which is beyond the boundaries of the known universe. Therefore, communion with nature is not so much for the sake of enjoying the natural as it is an important step in the visionary's journey toward new worlds elsewhere.[13]

Underlying Emerson's quest for environmental communion and for these new worlds is the notion of a benevolent universe. Nature must be the agent of harmony in the world, if one is to find spiritual fulfillment there. If one is to experience integration and redemption in the cosmos, then nature must not only be a receptacle of the divine, but it must also be receptive to the human. Emerson describes this nature as one that is never ill-disposed toward humanity and as one that presents itself as seducer and as the sacred object of reverence. "The stars awaken a certain reverence, . . . [and] Nature never wears a mean appearance."[14] Thus, for Emerson, nature is the sacred receptacle of the divine principle of goodness and beauty; it is the gentle and benevolent force that makes communion with alterity not only possible but desirable as well.[15]

Thus, nature rouses an attitude of reverence within the human imagination; but what is it about nature that, as Tony Tanner says, causes such an "admiration (wondering at)" of the natural world? Why is it that Emerson seeks to "enjoy an untrammeled intimacy with nature,"[16] and what is it about nature that makes it the object of desire for the genius or for the person with heightened vision? Emerson's naive eye recognizes the divine spirit in nature, and it is this recognition that lures the romantic visionary toward a closer intimacy with the natural receptacle of otherness. In other words, Emerson and the romantic poets do not desire communion with nature because of the succulent sweetness of nature itself. Nature is not seductive because of its own inherent worth or because of its own beauty. Rather, nature is worthy and captivating because of what lies within and beyond the natural world, and it fascinates because it is the medium through which human beings merge mystically with the wholly "other." In short, nature is the object of desire for the visionary poet because the natural world is hallowed ground that allows the union of humanity and deity through "*ascension,* or the passage of souls into higher forms."[17]

This higher end of nature points out the second way the romantic writers approach the natural. They desire not only to commune with the natural world but to transcend it as well. The real crux of the romantic worldview lies within this desire to ascend to higher forms of reality. The focus of the romantic poet is always ultimately the radical alterity that resides within or beyond the natural world. Thus, the romantic emphasis is otherworldly or at least transworldly. The Emersonian disciples, looking at the world through a sacred lens, find in it the footprints of the transcendent. They look to this world to find evidence of what lies beyond—they look to the world beyond that can be reached only through unity with nature. As a result, one can find in romantic writers both a monistic philosophy that joins Spirit and nature and an incipient dualism.

> Much romantic literature presupposes a double bifurcation. Existence is divided into two realms, heaven and earth, supernatural and natural, the "real" world and the derived world.[18]

The romantic poet reveres nature in order ultimately to move beyond the natural world to the reality of spirit. In this dualistic worldview, nature becomes a stepping-stone to otherness.

However, the romantic religious vision is not limited to the natural realm, for it also holds reverence for the social world. The "modernist impulse," which runs throughout nineteenth-century-liberal ideologies, assumes that God is immanent in culture and in human beings.[19] Thus, a second major tenet from the romantic tradition is that individuals in social relationships manifest spiritual worth as well as those in harmony with nature; human beings are inherently good and are receptacles for divine reality. The result of this positive anthropology is an unbounded optimism for the world of the nineteenth century. Progress was the theme for those who followed in the footsteps of the romantics and for nineteenth-century millenial groups in general, which sought to perfect the social realm.

The transcendentalists articulated their religious social vision in experimental social communes such as Fruitlands and Brook Farm. A short description of this transcendentalist urge toward social reform demonstrates how the romantic social vision paralleled the romantic natural world ideal. This examination of the transcendentalist attempt to create utopian communities aptly illustrates the second pole (the social pole) of the sacred American dream of possibility that filtered through and gained momentum from the romantic sacralization of natural and social space in America.

Brook Farm and Fruitlands were romantic reinterpretations of the Puritan sacred social mandate to create a "city upon a hill." George Ripley, the founder of Brook Farm, even wrote to Emerson and described his attempt at social reform as building "the 'city of God.'"[20] Ripley's idea of a city of God was to "establish social relations allowing freedom, growth, justice, and love."[21] Thus, human equality was the main goal of Ripley's social experiment from the beginning—equality that abolished "domestic servitude," that ended class distinction, and that allowed "the development of humanity . . . [into] holy men and women."[22] This idea of

radical equality was the driving force behind the transcendentalists' social experiments. Yet, what lies behind this desire for social
equality? What notion leads to the excess of Bronson Alcott at
Fruitlands, who disallowed consumption of "anything which
caused suffering or harm to any living creature?"[23] What fundamental principle guided the transcendentalists in their quest for
social reform?

The principle that led to radical ideas of social reform for the
transcendentalists was the same principle that led to their notions
of environmental communion and transcendence. The transcendentalists extended the romantic view of a sacred world to social
space and based their social theories upon the premises that the
human animal is the receptacle of the divine and that, therefore,
the social world is sacred.

This idea of a sacred social environment, which allows a residence for and access to otherness, was summarized nicely by
Elizabeth Peabody in a passage from *Dial*. In support of social experimentation, Peabody wrote that social structures should allow
the "divine principle in" men and women "to unfold itself," and
any society that does not support the divine nature of humanity is
"devilish."[24] For Peabody, and for the transcendentalist social re-
formers, the social world is sacred and should promote the eleva-
tion of human beings because they have in them a spark of the
divine.

This social view adds another dimension to the American
dream of possibility for a chosen people in a chosen land. This
dream, filtered through the romantic emphasis on transcendence,
emerged as a vision that focused upon an America that was made
up of a sacred physical and social world. Yet, this romantic approach to the world is one of profound confusion and disorientation. This worldview seems to emphasize the worth of the reality
of this world and of individuals and of the necessity of harmony
with both; however, upon closer examination, one discerns that
the true object of the romantic poet's desire is not this world, nature, or even the persons who inhabit this sacred realm. Rather,
the romantic worldview focuses upon that which is beyond this
world; nature and human beings are ultimately means to experience that spiritual, transcendent reality that resides in "a world
elsewhere."[25] As a result, the Emersonian approach to the world is
one in which transworldly connection is the goal—one that allows
the poet to "mount above these clouds and opaque airs" in order
to view reality "from the heaven of truth."[26]

This emphasis on otherworldliness and transcendence appears

throughout the writings of Emerson and Walt Whitman and occurs as the ability to obtain a heightened awareness—an "original
relation to the universe." Their concept of the poet, who alone enjoys this original relation, is perhaps the greatest development of
the idea of a divine humanity that can transcend mundane reality
to enjoy the unmediated encounter with alterity. It is the poet
who is able to transcend to ultimate reality through union with the
sacred natural and human realms. For Emerson,

> there is a property in the horizon which no man has but he whose eye
> can integrate all the parts, that is, the poet. . . . I become a transparent
> eyeball; I am nothing; I see; the currents of the Universal Being circu-
> late through me; I am part and parcel of God.[27]

This Emersonian transparent eyeball, which focuses upon
otherworldly reality, perhaps receives no greater development
than it does in the poetry and prose of Walt Whitman. Even
though Whitman stands at the intersection of romanticism and realism, he embodies the romantic emphasis upon the search for
the divine in the world. Whitman is reminiscent of Emerson in
"Song of Myself" when he celebrates nature and humanity. In this
celebration, he rejoices in such a small thing as a "leaf of grass
[that] is no less than the journey-work of the stars. . . ." Yet, like
Emerson, he does not revel in the natural for the sake of nature
itself. Rather, Whitman looks to nature, to "every object," and to
"the faces of men and women" in order to see what divine reality
the world unfolds.[28] It is the transworldly reality that receives the
praises of Whitman's song, and it is the otherness that resides in
people and in nature that lends the universe and all that is in it sacred significance.

A cluster of religious beliefs concerning America filtered
through the romantic tradition and emerged as a bipolar statement about America as a sacred world. America is sacred because
it allows possibility and because it contains otherness, and this sacred quality emerges both through the physical space of America
(the natural environment) and through its people (the social environment). These two poles of sacred America, the physical and
the social, developed in the nineteenth century around images of
American space. The sacred physical America was associated with
the expanding frontier and the democratic opportunity that it
represented, while the sacred social America emerged in symbolic
form as the city where opportunity abounded for all people.[29]
Both of these images of American space (the natural and the

social) failed by the end of the nineteenth century, and Americans were threatened by the appearance of a new, strange environment—one bereft of its familiar, sacred meaning.

The two poles of the American sacred dream shifted during the late nineteenth century and early twentieth century as thinkers and writers exorcised the supernatural from both the physical and social world and articulated a secularized spatial environment. However, this restructuring of America's symbols did not destroy the American dream of possibility and its religious quality. Rather, it rendered it in a new form that, although secular, would still impart meaning to an environment that had lost its sacred footing. This transition of natural and social space from sacred to secular status occurred as the nineteenth century became the twentieth, and it resulted in a fundamental redefinition of American space as spiritually and morally significant.

2. Redefinition: From Sacred to Secular America

Despite the sharp contrast between sacred and secular understandings of environment in American culture around the turn of the century, one can detect a measure of continuity within the exchange of the two. Both orientations conceive environment (space) as otherness—as the "not me." This ingredient lends the redefinition and the reassessment of environment in American culture a real, albeit muted, religious quality. Indeed, the ability of culture to undergo so radical a change is due to what Giles Gunn calls the confrontation with otherness. When one encounters the "not me," whether through literary expression or religious experience, one faces the possibility of world alteration or world creation. It is this occasion that prompts the search for meaning and the questioning of commonly held assumptions about one's world. When new patterns of thought, meaning, and significance are provided, whether in religious or in literary terms, it is because the confrontation with otherness provides entrance to a world of possibility—the world of the unknown—the redefined world to be.[30] In other words, an encounter with otherness is metaphysically crucial when a fundamental change occurs in the way people view their world. The encounter with the "not me" is existentially meaningful when it moves from threat of alienation to a whole new way of thinking about and seeing the world.

Such an experience of alterity, which occasions a worldview redefinition, describes the development of nineteenth-century liter-

ature. Examples of literature that seemed to participate in the
redefinition of American space began to surface in the romantic
tradition as M. H. Abrams has shown. Abrams, in *Natural Supernaturalism,* describes the way in which the romantic writers attempted worldview redefinition by seeking "to naturalize the
supernatural and to humanize the divine."[31] This strategy attempted to save a declining worldview by creating a world where
the supernatural existed in the natural realm and where the
"other" could be experienced through the social world. Nevertheless, these efforts were insufficient for the romantics to participate
in the process of worldview redefinition, because even though supernatural categories of description changed in their language,
they still asserted the traditional search for unification with the
transcendent.[32] All that differed for the romantic writers was that
they sought the supernatural through the natural and social
realms.

Among the developments that undermined the romantic worldview and that secularized the American natural and social environment, one stands out as particularly forceful. The Darwinian
revolution, as Perry Miller points out, forced a worldview redefinition in American culture as the nineteenth century came to a close.
Miller asserts that the latter third of the nineteenth century witnessed "one of the most radical revolutions in the history of the
American mind."[33] While the way Americans conceived their position in the universe was changed forever by two revolutionary
philosophies that invaded ideological America, Hegelian idealism
and Darwinian naturalism, the second of these was decisive in
bringing about a demise of and the need for redefinition of romantic spatial orientations.

In Miller's estimation, the single most profound challenge to
American identity came in the form of evolutionary thought as
developed by Herbert Spencer's social naturalism. The whole-
hearted reception of Spencer's philosophy was made possible by
the revolutionary effect Darwin had on popular America. The
point of Miller's book is that whether or not one resonates with
the Darwinian worldview, the post-1859 American had to play the
game of world construction by Darwin's rules.[34] When Darwin
published *The Origin of Species* in 1859, he brought to a festering
head and gave form to a cluster of enlightenment ideas that had
floundered helplessly in America for a century. After 1859, the
popular mind in America wrestled with an alien and unfamiliar
world conception as evolutionary thought affected and changed
the way Americans perceived their religious, ideological, and cultural institutions. No area of popular America was left untouched

by the Darwinian revolution, and after 1859, Americans struggled with the uncertainty of world disintegration.

Post-Darwinian Americans lost the familiar worldview of "their parents and preceptors," according to Granville Hicks,[35] at a time when disturbance and the unexpected characterized American religion. This was hardly a period of religious, cultural, and political stability, but the crisis created by Darwinian theory had a particularly radical consequence for American life when compared to other changes and conflicts distressing public life in the country. It severed the dependence of cultural values on inherited, although reinterpreted and muted, religious beliefs. The consequence was fundamental and world-shattering for American religion and culture. Ferenc Szasz, in *The Divided Mind of Protestant America, 1880–1930,* elaborates on the mounting tension between religion and culture as he focuses on the seminal influence that the evolution controversy exerted upon religion and society from the 1860s through the 1920s. A closer look at Szasz's work helps to illuminate the severance that a Darwinian world caused between traditional religion and American culture at the turn of the century.[36]

Szasz argues that a major cultural transformation took place during the latter nineteenth and early twentieth centuries. In 1880 Protestant hegemony characterized American society; however, by 1930, Protestantism split apart, its hold on American culture disappeared, and secularization and pluralism characterized American society instead of Protestantism. Protestantism was no longer the focal point of American culture but was simply one cultural manifestation among many in a religiously pluralistic society. Consequently, cultural values could no longer find their sponsor, guide, or ground in Protestantism.

Szasz attributes this change to conflicts within Protestantism, which ensued during these years, as well as to the conflict between Protestant Christianity and the surrounding culture. In the latter part of the nineteenth century, theological issues such as evolution and biblical higher criticism began to divide Protestant Christians into conservative and liberal camps. Thus, Protestantism divided more along conservative-liberal lines than along denominational lines. The result was that practically all Protestant groups in America had two antagonistic pockets that were either conservative or liberal. Szasz contends that this polarization culminated in the Fundamentalist-Modernist controversy of the 1920s. The divided house of Protestantism, which created hostility often more important than denominational differences, contributed to the demise of Protestant hegemony and to the rise of secularization.

Szasz's analysis of how conservatives and liberals responded to progressive ideas in the early twentieth century is especially insightful. Szasz rebels against the predominant notion that only the liberals rallied in support of progressivism and social action. Rather, both conservatives and liberals participated in the progressive spirit, but they did so in different ways. For a while, at least, the fierce theological debates of the latter nineteenth century were toned down as each faction turned its energy to social action; however, as the progressive spirit diminished, so did the last vestiges of Protestant hegemony. Conservatives and liberals once again turned their antagonisms toward one another, and the rise of secular notions flourished as Protestantism suffered.

Szasz consolidates his theses concerning the breakdown of Protestantism's cultural authority in his discussion of the Fundamentalist-Modernist controversy. This controversy began around 1920 as a theological dispute over biblical authority; however, it quickly shifted direction and reverted back to the old question of evolution. This clash over evolution came to a head and to maturity in the Scopes trial, which highlighted the different worldviews of the modernists and fundamentalists. In many ways, says Szasz, the fundamentalist movement was a revolt by the common person who tried to hold on to a last remnant of legitimacy through religion—a religion that made humankind the center and object of a divinely created world of transcendent immanence. The security they found in this religious approach to reality disappeared with the advent of modern scientific approaches to religion.

Szasz's argument is important to this study because it highlights the ontological threat that cultural and religious trends held for the nineteenth-century American. Traditional Christian beliefs, which pictured a God residing in a world where individuals were of prime importance, were under siege by the onslaught of scientific and secular visions of reality that gained prominence in the latter nineteenth and early twentieth centuries. Religious identity, security, and sense of place were threatened, and the pressure brought to bear on traditional religious beliefs was only increased by such other rapid, world-altering events as industrialization, urbanization, and immigration. The effect of these unsettling events was one of estrangement and dislocation—the sense of Americans that they were chosen people in a promised land suffered questioning as the garden of promise became the battlefield of ideological conflicts.

However, Darwinism challenged more than the religion of the time and the American's sense of place. Cultural traditions experienced a period of uncertainty, also. The literature of the latter nineteenth and early twentieth centuries is in many ways the cultural expression of the American's estrangement. To fully understand what this estrangement entails, it is necessary to chronicle the American view of America as it changed in the literature of the nineteenth century. Leo Marx's *Machine in the Garden* and Henry Nash Smith's *The Virgin Land* are two classics in the field of American studies that continue to inform scholars of these changes that occurred in this crucial time of America's maturation. They both chronicle America's transition from sacred to secular self-descriptive categories—a transition that destroyed the garden myth of America.

Before Darwin's epoch making writings reached the popular mind in America, the governing literary image of American space revolved around the understanding of America as a sacred garden; it was a garden because America was the land that God created and challenged with a special purpose; America was sacred because the New World was the meeting place of God and human beings. It was within this garden that pre-1859 Americans found God; therefore, it is not surprising that early imagery concerning America revolved around allusions to the Garden of Eden—the paradisiacal garden where God and human both walked. The garden of America was sacred space in two different ways. It represented a sacred and paradisiacal natural world; however, it also symbolized a sacred social world where people could aspire to live without sin and in total harmony with one another.

Henry Nash Smith identifies the importance that the natural garden myth played in the development of America. As the Wild West was domesticated, the myth of the garden grew and eventually became the most influential factor in American settlement. The West and Northwest evolved as the "garden of the world" and magnetically attracted hordes to the promised land that God had created for Americans.[37] It is easy to see that natural America appeared to be the pinnacle of God's creation and the residence for God's people by examining the writings of some of America's early personalities. For example, Smith refers to Robert T. Walker and to Stephen Douglas to suggest that for early Americans, America's unity and greatness was the result of God's favor and creative pleasure. For Smith, the first three quarters of the nineteenth century shaped the character of America through the "relation between man and nature" as it developed in God's sacred garden of the American West.[38]

Borrowing the Turner thesis, Smith describes the West as the garden of the world that mystically attracted Americans. This pastoral image of America gave sacred significance to the land, because it was in the garden that God and humanity met face to face. In other words, the American land was sacred because it was here that one could experience the vital potentialities of human experience through an unmediated confrontation with otherness.

This sacred conception of the American garden is more fully developed in Leo Marx's *Machine in the Garden,* and it takes on a social twist as the garden myth falls in prominence. The idea that America is the sacred meeting place for God and humanity is the basis of Marx's depiction of the nineteenth-century environment as the pastoral ideal. For Marx, the pastoral idea, which is the harmonious relationship between civilization and nature, defines America. Furthermore, it is this pastoral conception of American space that allows for the "sensuous intimacy" between human beings and the "other."[39] In other words, in the first part of the nineteenth century, the American continent was sacred space, for it was in the garden that God walked and allowed human access—it was in the garden where man and woman lived in perfect peace and harmony.

Marx traces the pastoral ideal through world literature and early colonial developments; however, its dominance as the image of the American ideal did not begin until the latter part of the eighteenth century in the writings of Thomas Jefferson and persisted for about a century until the latter part of the nineteenth century. The pastoral ideal grew out of Jefferson's agrarian dream and his understanding of the "middle state . . . between the savage and the refined." The garden of America was not the wild frontier but this middle state, and for Jefferson, it made possible the best environment for Americans—the "new Eden." Jefferson and agrarian America operated on the assumption that a metaphysical link existed between nature and humanity. Thus, the predominant understanding of America in the first three-quarters of the 1800s came in terms of a peaceful garden where men and women lived in the presence of the transcendent—a peaceful garden that was a natural and social paradise.[40]

Nevertheless, the garden myth did not persist, and by the end of the nineteenth century, Americans were losing their grip on their paradisiacal world. Jefferson foresaw this likelihood in light of the War of 1812: "Our enemy has indeed the consolation of Satan on removing our first parents from Paradise: from a peaceable and agricultural nation, he makes us a military and manufacturing one."[41] There is no doubt that the garden myth fell from prominence in the latter half of the nineteenth century; Jefferson attributed this demise to war while Marx blames it on the intrusion of the machine into the garden. For Marx, industrialization undermined the sacred conception of the American natural and social garden.

Furthermore, industrialization caused a shift in the spatial setting for the dream of opportunity from the frontier to the city. Such a dream was embedded in the architectural interest in urban space at the World's Columbian Exposition of 1893 in Chicago. Yet, soon after the city called forth a promise of a new prosperity for America, it began to betray these hopes with the overcrowding, slums, and poverty that met workers who had followed the beckon of a new dream of American possibility. With the disappointment that industrialization helped to create, the hope of a new social world began to pass away, much as the hope for a natural sacred world had ended with the closing of the frontier. By the end of the nineteenth century, Americans lost all expectation of a sacred land that promised possibility for all; both the garden myth that promised the beauty of an unspoiled nature and the vision of a perfect society disintegrated.

Industrialization played a major role in this desacralization of American space; however, as Henry Nash Smith suggests, the real force behind the destruction of the garden myth ran much deeper. Smith refers to Edward Eggleston who suggests that the deterministic notions of Darwin stripped nature and humanity of their spiritual and metaphysical values.[42] In addition and in relation to this, Smith traces the loss of the sacrality of American space through the decline of the Leatherstocking hero. This hero was ineffectual in the latter part of the nineteenth century because Americans could no longer look for "God through nature, for nature . . . [was] no longer benign." The hero became isolated— "alone in a hostile, or at best a neutral universe."[43] Thus, the desacralization of American space was not simply a result of industrialization. The ills of industrialization were symptomatic of a larger, deeper, and more disturbing experience of alienation and isolation—the experience of post-Darwinian Americans.

The Darwinian revolution of the late nineteenth and early twentieth centuries joined with other forces to change not only scholarly thought but also the popular mind. After Darwin, Americans would find it increasingly difficult to view their world as the paradisiacal garden created for them. Gradually, men and women found themselves in a world where the Creator no longer ruled benevolently—a world that was indifferent to the needs of human beings and that was sometimes hostile to humanity. In other words, America was no longer the garden where God (the transcendent) and human beings could meet, but instead became a world that presented *itself* as wholly "other." Thus, Darwinian theory changed the way Americans thought about the human ontological status in relation to alterity.

This conceptual transition of American space from sacred ground to radical alterity had an alienating effect upon Americans that Perry Miller attributes to the invasion of German philosophy.[44] Furthermore, the Spencerian phase of this invasion gained popular audience through Darwinism. Why was the Darwinian revolution so unsettling and world shattering? Darwin's influence cannot be explained solely in terms of his presentation of a new scientific worldview; Enlightenment ideas were not new. Rather, Darwin's unsettling influence is important in America because it became an extension of Spencerian determinism and, thus, governed the human social world as well as the natural. This disturbing concept contributed a new way to think about the world and one's place in that world.[45]

Thus, the Darwinian intrusion into the popular mind of the nineteenth century attacked the ontological status of Americans. According to Miller, Darwin reduced human beings to the level of the animals, and his theory was not only a "threat to traditional morality" but also an ontological threat that attacked "the very conception of humanity."[46] *The Origin of Species* was epoch making because after Darwin, humanity could no longer consider itself the center of God's creation. Rather, humans were just another species on the periphery of existence, vying for survival by employing their superior physical and mental capacities in both their natural and their social environments. As a result, the Darwinian revolution, in a primarily Spencerian form, occasioned a fundamental deconstruction of the way Americans thought about and responded to their world.

3. The Redefinition of American Space and the American Mind

The decline of the pastoral ideal and sacred ideas concerning America in the nineteenth century was a part of this revolutionary change in the way Americans perceived their place in the world. Nineteenth-century America experienced the horror of dislocation—they lost the World that gave legitimacy to their existence. However, this dislocation was not altogether negative, but it led as well to a reconstruction of the American worldview and to relocation within a meaningful environment. In fact, a premise of this study is that dislocation must occur if meaningful location is to result. I shall explore the possibilities of this thesis for American literature in chapter 4.

Nevertheless, this dislocation did occur and nineteenth-century Americans lost their familiar sacred worldview. This change surfaced in all areas of American life. Economically, capitalism and industrialization were allowed to change the face of the American garden permanently. Socially, the overcrowding of cities destroyed the pastoral ideal for millions. Politically, the Populist Revolt expressed the frustration of those farmers who witnessed the end of agrarian America—an America that drew its life from the garden myth.[47] Religiously, the debate over evolution and creationism preoccupied the Protestant mind in America until the Scopes trial in the 1920s.[48] Finally, through the arts (in this case literature) a new American environment—a redefined spatial orientation—emerged through the sponsorship of realism and naturalism.

The literature of the latter nineteenth and early twentieth centuries participated in the redefinition of the American environment in response to the Darwinian revolution; however, this literature also helped to extend the Darwinian revolution to the popular level. Thus, the literature of the late nineteenth century and the early twentieth century not only reflects cultural patterns but also anticipates and participates in cultural change. The realistic and naturalistic literary movements in America prepared the way for the twentieth-century literature of disillusionment and alienation by positing a profane or secular America. Through the desacralization of American space—through stripping away the metaphysical ground between humanity and the transcendent— American realistic and naturalistic literature defined the rise of a twentieth-century secular nation.[49]

The realists achieved a worldview redefinition by rejecting the fundamental goal of both traditional theology and the romantic tradition. The realists denied that one need reunite with the transcendent and that the supernatural could even exist in the natural or social world. With this fundamental denial of supernatural presence within the world, the exponents of late nineteenth-century literature redefined the sacred worldview inherited by and passed along by the romantics; they completed a transition from viewing America as sacred to viewing America as a secular, but still meaningful, place. The goal of this study is to demonstrate how this shift took place and to describe the belief structures accompanying it.

The examination of Willa Cather and Theodore Dreiser within the scope of this goal may at first seem to be an ill-fated attempt to weave a whole where only fragments and patches are pieced together. Indeed, in the minds of many, Cather and Dreiser have nothing in common save the fact that the first three decades of the present century witnessed the blossoming of their classic but often overlooked careers. Yet, they share in the realistic and naturalistic redefinition of the American environment. Upon closer examination, which this study attempts to provide, areas of congruity between these two writers continue to arise and bother the literary critic. These bothersome areas of correlation are not mere accidents. Rather, they indicate that the narratives of Dreiser and Cather participate in a common activity—they redefine American space in the latter nineteenth and early twentieth centuries. What Cather's fiction explores in terms of the natural and physical landscape of American heartland, Dreiser's fiction explores in the spaces of the American urban cityscape.

Cather's and Dreiser's life and work encompass a time that represented an important crossroads for America—a time when Americans began to think of their land in secular terms rather than in sacred categories—a time when Americans both lost and regained a meaningful world. Cather and Dreiser are important because they were both affected by and participated in the process of world destruction and reconstruction—in the redefinition of American space from sacred to secular.

This process of redefinition occurred when Americans were dislocated—when their world no longer disclosed otherness but became "other" and alien to them. This experience of alterity occasioned a radical reassessment of the sacred world in the realistic tradition, as when the characters in the works of such authors as Cather and Dreiser attempt to come to terms with their environment. For example, in Cather's works, alterity occurs on the prairie and the western frontier, while in Dreiser's work, this radical alterity comes in the form of the urban environment. In both cases, the environment, which presents itself as "other," suffers redefinition concerning basic cultural attitudes about that environment. In Cather's fiction, the sacred West suffers secularization, and in Dreiser's fiction, the benevolent assumptions about social space fall to the hauntingly realistic picture of perverse human relationships. Because the supernatural is cast out of the world, whether in the natural or social environment, the works of Cather and Dreiser are typical of the literary situation of the time and of the newly conceived environment.

The one aspect of this secularizing tendency in American fiction that is common to both Cather and Dreiser (and to much of the realistic and naturalistic traditions) is the estrangement of characters within this unfamiliar or hostile environment. However, this rise of the hostile environment is not limited to American realism. In a study on nineteenth-century English literature, Lee T. Lemon attempts to establish a similar pattern that centers around the mid-century Darwinian phenomenon. In the literature of the early part of the century, nature and the world appear as beneficent; however, by the end of the century, characters in English novels (especially in Hardy's work) appear in "an indifferent or hostile universe."[50] It is my contention that the same type of pattern exists in nineteenth-century and early twentieth-century American literature, and that Cather's and Dreiser's works demonstrate this transition to antagonistic settings in American realism.

Furthermore, this pattern of a developing hostile universe both mirrors and helps to create a cultural belief and mood of Americans that results, in part, from the popularization of Darwinian and Spencerian doctrine, the closing of the frontier, and the rise of the industrial city. These events conspired to create an America that made Americans strangers in their own world and that challenged long accepted beliefs about the American mission in the new world. This experience of estrangement caused a confrontation with radically new ways to view America and to gain meaning, and the experimentation with these new forms of meaning through fiction contributed greatly to the redefinition of American space in the nineteenth century.

The encounter with such an unknown world results, as Giles Gunn suggests, in facing the vital potentialities of that alien world and, thus, in world redefinition. Such is true for a few of the characters in Cather's and Dreiser's fiction. These characters are visionary[51] in that they face radical alterity (imposed upon them by their environment), and they are able to forge a new understanding of the world and how it works—they assimilate new patterns of thinking and meaning. These characters, when confronted with the Darwinian world and with the destruction of their familiar environment, construct new ways of seeing the world as occasioning moral and spiritual possibilities. Americans at the end of the nineteenth century approximate these characters, because they also existed in an existentially threatening world of Darwinian and Spencerian indifference and could no longer approach existence and relationships in traditional ways—they could no longer seek communion with the supernatural in their familiar and benevolent universe. But how did they move from this experience of estrangement to an ability to assimilate new patterns of thinking and meaning? The transition affected the natural, social, religious, and literary worlds and it did so through a general pattern that moves one from a situation of dislocation to a place of relocation.

The move from dislocation to reappropriation is fundamental for Timothy Bauer-Yocum in his work on Walt Whitman and Henry Adams. Through his study, Bauer-Yocum identifies a three-fold pattern of changing attitudes toward American meaning that helps to set the stage for this study of Cather and Dreiser. From his readings in American studies Bauer-Yocum isolates the following stages: (1) first, there is a "period of naive affirmation" when traditions continue intact; (2) second, there exists a "period of disillusionment and sense of crisis" when confusion reigns and the traditions are rejected; and (3) finally, there is a "movement toward recovery and reassessment of the meaning of America and of personal life within the context of that meaning."[52]

This same pattern of rejection and reassessment emerges throughout the scholarly tradition of American studies. For example, even the organizational pattern of Giles Gunn's collection of readings in American religious history, *New World Metaphysics,* suggests such a pattern. His first four sections, entitled "Presentiments," "Preparations," "Loomings," and "Realizations," describe the building of and realization of American identity. The last two sections, entitled "Rejections and Revisions" and "Recoveries," describe the process of loss of that identity and then the reassessment of the outmoded notions in a way that allows them to make sense in a changing time.[53]

This three-fold pattern of innocence, rejection, and reassessment is exactly the process that I claim for the redefinition of American space in the literature of Willa Cather and Theodore Dreiser. In the nineteenth century, both the romantic era and the post-Darwin enthusiasm represent two eras of innocence when two conflicting worldviews gained wide acceptance. However, the fiction of Cather and Dreiser question these worldviews, reject them, and redefine them in a way that expels the supernatural from the natural and social worlds and that secularizes American space that was once sacred. Thus, for those who wonder why two

writers like Cather and Dreiser should be yoked together for the
purposes of a study in the transformation of the American moral
and spiritual vision, it should be said that they, in their own ways,
unknowingly cooperate in the redefinition of space as morally
and spiritually significant.[54]

Willa Cather and Theodore Dreiser represent two manifestations of the secularization of American space, and they participate
in the negation of the bipolar (natural and social poles) sacred
worldview. Cather's fiction secularizes the sacred understanding
of natural space and redefines the Garden Myth, while Dreiser's
fiction negates the sacred understanding of social America. With
their fiction, the sacred world of the romantic poets undergoes
scrutiny, rejection, and redefinition; the result is an America
whose sacred symbols shift to secular bulwarks. With Cather and
Dreiser, the secularization of American space in the literature of
the early twentieth century is complete.

The religious and cultural traditions from the middle of the
nineteenth century through the first two decades of the twentieth
century are pivotal to the history and culture of America. This era
marks the maturity of a new nation; the rise of an agrarian state
to a manufacturing and a military superpower; the loss of cultural
homogeneity and the rise of a pluralistic society; and the demise
of a sacred worldview and the birth of a secular America. Standing at this crucial junction in American history are Willa Cather
and Theodore Dreiser, and they deserve attention because of
their role in bringing about a redefinition of American space. The
redefinition of American space from a sacred to a secular world
marks a crucial phase in the development of American identity
and self understanding, and it, therefore, carries ethical and ontological import. As a result, no cultural, religious, moral, or social
form remains unscathed by this transformation of the American
mind.

In particular, literary forms function to help build the American mind, because they constitute a type of cultural expression
that possesses a connection to religious belief. I hope to show that
what people think religiously about their place in the cosmos sur-
faces in and is shaped by narrative through the relationship of the
elements of setting and character. Therefore, while I deal with
the particular fictions of the latter part of the nineteenth century
and the early part of the twentieth century, I am searching for a
continuing American mode of thought (as it concerns one's place
within the world)—an "American mind"—during that same era.
By doing this I hope to expose a point of connection between

American literature and the American religious imagination. If religion and literature enjoy any inherent relationship, it is because they both emerge from the same ontological base. In fact, the literary form allows the reader to experience the wider, cultural situation in a concentrated form; therefore, religion and culture are related dialectically within fiction, and each influences the other. "The fictions become crucibles forging or discovering wholes in a situation which appears to be broken."[55]

This work is a critique of the fiction of two significant American writers at the beginning of this century; it is a study of the force that the narrative element of atmosphere or setting exerts upon the depiction and development of character; it is an examination of the relationship between religion and literature; it is a search for an "American mind" of the period. However, first and foremost, it is a description of a cultural redefinition of American space—a redefinition that exchanged a romantic philosophy of sacred space, which views the world as a secondary entity or a means to otherness, for a secularized version of American space, which regards the world as a primary entity where space itself is otherness. The tension between these two worldviews is not confined to the turbulent beginnings of the 1900s, but it continues to haunt American religious identity as this century turns its sights toward the next. Thus, as I turn toward this examination of Cather, Dreiser, and the American religious imagination, I do so with the hope that this work, which is rooted historically in the last century, may inform our own struggles in the present as we look to the future and wrestle with questions of sacred and secular America.

2

Living on the Edge of a World

Willa Cather's Alien Frontiers and the Antagonism of Place

Where the sacred world of the romantic poets provided a benevolent natural world that was a gateway to otherness, Willa Cather's fiction reflects a reversal of this understanding of environment. With Cather's fiction, one witnesses the destruction of the American dream associated with natural space. Natural America, particularly the West, could no longer be viewed as a Garden of Eden or as the special place where God would carry out his mission. America became instead an alienating and harsh world symbolized by Cather's frontier. It is this alienating frontier that makes Cather's characters marginal and dislocated within a strange world, and it is this frontier that allows those characters to overcome their marginality by developing proper human relationships within a culturally and ethnically complex situation.

1. Introduction to Cather's Fiction and the Ambiguity of Theme

The midwestern frontier, the Nebraska plains, and the desert Southwest dominate the fiction of Willa Cather. These settings should not be surprising, because Cather's biography reveals the dominant role that the western move across the American continent played in her own life. When she was a young girl, her family ventured beyond their Winchester, Virginia, home to seek a new life and promised opportunities "out West" near Red Cloud, Nebraska. With Nebraska in the background, her own pioneering experience provides the backdrop for the western settings of her novels and short stories.[1] Thus, it is natural for many critics, like E. K. Brown, to assert that "Willa Cather was under the spell of the Nebraska countryside" that was at the core of her fiction.[2]

Drawing from her own experiences on the prairie, Cather wrote not only about the pioneers, the immigrants, and the colorful characters that filled her life and her pages; rather, she wrote first and foremost about "the clash of character and environment"—the struggle between the pioneer and the frontier setting that is primarily in her prairie novels.[3] Furthermore, Cather's fiction is at its best when it deals primarily with this frontier environment that is, for Cather, "the essence of life in America."[4] Because of the centrality of the frontier setting in Cather's work, an examination of setting is crucial to a study on Cather. This is not to suggest that the other literary elements—character, plot, and tone—are not important; rather, it is to suggest that setting tends to dominate the majority of Cather's work. It is Cather's fictional environment that sets the agenda for what is possible in her stories. In other words, setting places constraints upon and grants possibilities to the characters and to the action within Cather's fictional world.[5]

The role of setting and natural space in Cather's fiction develops from two perspectives. First, Cather's work redefines natural space in light of the romantic worldview. Where the sacred world of the romantic poets provided a benevolent natural world that was a gateway to otherness, Willa Cather's fiction reflects a reversal of this understanding of environment. With Cather, the frontier is an unfamiliar, often hostile reality that is an impediment to personal fulfillment. Thus, the frontier is not a familiar or friendly place that beckons one to it and beyond it; as a result pioneers are marginal creatures—characters who are caught between worlds where they do not belong. The American natural world can no longer be viewed as the sacred world of the romantics. America, the garden, is instead an alienating and harsh world symbolized by Cather's frontier.

Second, Cather's fiction redefines the Darwinian worldview. Even though Cather's characters are often dominated by their environment, Cather's fiction does not describe a strictly deterministic or naturalistic environment; Cather is never quite comfortable with Darwin's world. As harsh as the frontier seems, it is not a world that is governed solely by the law of the survival of the fittest; rather, it is a world where human qualities other than physical strength make a difference. As a result, Cather's fiction carves a new worldview out of its response to and redefinition of two competing worldviews—the romantic sacred conception of the world and the Darwinistic, naturalistic world construction. This new worldview is a secularized conception of American natural space, which emerges from Cather's ambivalence toward her own dominant perspectives on space, and this secularized view departs from both the romantic and naturalistic attitudes toward America.

Cather's attitude toward the natural space and the physical environment, then, is an ambivalent one and issues in her unique presentation of both the natural and physical worlds. This ambivalence is represented best by two attitudes or poles in Cather's reconstruction of the American landscape. The first pole is negative and presents itself in the form of a landscape that is stifling and limiting—the landscape that develops as Cather redefines the romantic sacred conception of the world. The second pole is positive and relates the land as that which has the power to liberate. This pole emerges as Cather's fiction explores the world that exists beyond Darwin's world of natural selection. Yet, within this ambivalence between a stifling land and a liberating land, there is an inclusive pattern that grants Cather's conception of natural space legitimacy through a secularized, or desacralized, notion of the world. Therefore, the ambiguities present here are not simply the artistic expressions of her own confused vision, as most critics seem to assert, but vital representatives of Cather's unified worldview.

2. Willa Cather's Ambiguous Conception of Natural Space

The dominant scholarly perception of Cather's fiction, as clearly evidenced in the criticism of Sister Lucy Schneider, C.S.J., suggests that no pattern exists in Cather's ambiguous land philosophy because of the fundamental tension between reality and transcendence in Cather's work. On the one hand, human beings are tied to this world much as captives are chained to their captor. On the other hand, this world (the land) can also lead to transcendence much as the romantic poets celebrated in their quest for a pathway to otherness through the means of nature. Thus, Cather's fiction portrays the natural world as ambiguous—it frustrates and enslaves its inhabitants, yet it provides the possibility (or at least hope) for a meaningful encounter with otherness.

The land is at once frustrating and liberating; harsh and salvific; stifling and enabling. Schneider illustrates this through an examination of Cather's early short stories. In particular, she contrasts "Lou, the Prophet" and "The Clemency of the Court."

In the first story, the land operates to isolate and confine, while in the second story, the land is the sacred ground where one transcends the ordinary world. Furthermore, Schneider asserts that Cather's attitude toward the land shifted throughout her career, and she finds consistency in this ambivalence only in relation to Cather's personal status as an artist. For example, she claims that Cather's early short stories "enumerate the faults of the land and reject its offer of close association" and mirror turbulence in her personal life, while Cather's middle and later creative periods reflect the positive, harmonious, and liberating aspects of the land and of Cather's life.[6] Schneider asserts that "the land is good in itself by *nature*, but . . . it can seem to be evil in its *operations*."[7] Thus, Schneider says that Cather uses the land as something that is divided against itself—something that has an essence different from its existence.

This view of the land in Cather's work, as something that is ambiguous in and of itself, is not uncommon among Cather scholars. Thus, in the critical reception, natural space in Cather's novels appears as unreliable. The unreliable land beckons humanity to it with the promise of transcendence and opportunity, yet it entraps those who seek this deliverance through it. It is as if there are "two visions of nature" in Cather's fiction; one is tame and inviting while the other vision appears as bitter and twisted.[8] However, this view is flawed from at least three perspectives. First, it is clear that natural space in Cather's novels appears as ambiguous; however, contrary to the popular critical opinion, it is not the land itself that is unreliable. Rather, it is the human manipulation of and approach to the land that determines whether or not natural space is liberating or confining. It is only the human despoliation of the natural world that ruins the liberating aspects of nature and that makes nature a prison. I shall examine this more fully in the section of this chapter on Cather's redefinition of the romantic worldview.

Secondly, while critics notice and describe this tension, they often fail to recognize the unity within it—a unity that lies at the heart of Cather's redefinition of sacred conceptions of the land. It is only because Americans focus on the land as sacred that this tension exists. The promises of transcendence connected with the sacred view of nature frustrate only because the sacred orientation is no longer sufficient. Thus, Cather's ambiguity is not a flaw or inconsistency but an entirely consistent and patterned way of presenting the failure of an outdated worldview, the sacred, and exchanging it for a revised worldview, the secular.

The third point at which the critical reception of Cather's ambiguity fails is with the comparison of the uncivilized and the civilized natural world.[9] For example, Schneider distinguishes between the wild land and the humanized land in Cather's work; however, she places them on the same level and sees both wildness and tameness as important elements in one's struggle for transcendence. The challenge of transcendence is to overcome otherness and to humanize it. This theme is developed by Cather in her middle and later fiction, according to Schneider. For example, *O Pioneers!* is in resonance with Whitman's "Pioneers! O Pioneers!" that celebrates the conquest of the Western boundaries of America.

Nevertheless, according to Schneider, the wildness of this western land is positive when redeemed by the civilizing influence of culture, and for Schneider, there is little difference between natural and civilized land. For example, the virginal Southwest is redeemed only when Father Latour imposes form upon the native rock and builds a magnificent cathedral. Thus, for Schneider, unspoiled natural space and humanized natural space exist together in Cather's fiction to create a unified "land philosophy."[10] As a result, the difference between "natural" land and humanized space is not a difference of essence but one of role and degree. Other critics deal with this comparison of wild land to civilized space in temporal terms rather than in spatial. For example, many critics dichotomize the land of the ancient people with the frontier of the pioneers and state that Cather views the past nostalgically. Thus, they minimize the role of environment and make it subservient to time in Cather's work.[11]

I wish to approach the comparison of wildness and civilization in a different way. Unlike Schneider, I shall make a radical distinction between natural land and civilized land. These entities do not simply differ in their role or in degree; rather, humanized land is radically, essentially different from unspoiled land. A mythical and lost virginal land once carried sacred significance, but the civilizing process stripped that natural space of its sacred character. Furthermore, unlike critics such as Granville Hicks, I hope to deal with the sense of place in Cather's work without diminishing its role to that of temporality. The difference between ancient land and the frontier land is not a difference of time alone; rather, it is a difference in the human attitude toward the land.

It is in response to Cather's ambivalent attitude toward the land that I formulate my understanding of the sense of space in Cather's work. In Cather's work, the land is no longer the gateway to otherness as it was for the romantic poets before her; therefore, the natural world is not something to be transcended or overcome. Yet, to overcome the land is precisely what the pioneer struggle, about which she so often writes, is all about. The pioneer fails to recognize the land as the natural world that cannot be tamed—as otherness itself. With the pioneer's failure to approach the natural world as "other" came the secularizing influence that the settling of the frontier brought, and the frontier was secularized by the attitude and actions of pioneer inhabitants. In contrast to this secularized space is the picture of the natural world in its harmonious state as it appears in relation to the ancient Indian Cliff Dweller in the desert Southwest (which has yet to be tamed for Cather). This natural and unspoiled state of the land is not virginal solely because it came earlier in time; rather, it is the remnant of a certain human response to the land in its natural state. The first approach refuses to recognize the land as "other" and conquers the land, modernizes it, and secularizes natural space. The second approach to the natural world recognizes the otherness of the land and reveres it in a way to preserve its natural harmony.

Thus, the ambiguity toward the land in Cather's work revolves around two different patterns or models for natural and physical space. In one model, physical space is imposed upon and suffers the effects of secularization. This is reflected by the frontier (usually in the Midwest) in Cather's stories after the pioneer has tamed the land. The second model is a natural space that has not suffered from the human need to dominate and appears in Cather's fiction usually in the Southwest, where Cather makes an intimate connection between harmony with the natural world and intimacy in human relationships. The way one approaches the land in Cather's fiction causes reciprocal consequences for human relationships. Thus, if a character devotes all of his or her energy to taming the land, it is usually at the expense of meaningful relationships. Conversely, a character may have a healthy and harmonious relationship with environment when he or she also enjoys strong and meaningful relationships with other human beings. Unfortunately, this is what a majority of Willa Cather's characters fail to realize and incorporate in their lives.

To unravel Cather's ambivalence toward natural space requires an examination of the two concepts of space that cause tension in her fiction. Through such an examination, it is possible to demonstrate that Cather was neither a romanticist nostalgically looking to the past and imposing sacred categories on the land, nor a naturalist resigning her characters to a hopeless existence in a deterministic universe. Rather, she describes the collapse of the American myth concerning the natural space that was consumed by the American westward expansion. This heroic enterprise did not occur without a price—the price was the loss of sacred America.

3. Expulsion From the Garden: Willa Cather's Redefinition of the Romantic World

Cather's preface to *O Pioneers!* hints at the dialogue that her fiction carries on with the romantic, sacral worldview.

PRAIRIE SPRING

> Evening and the flat land,
> Rich and sombre and always silent;
> The miles of fresh-plowed soil,
> Heavy and black, full of strength and harshness;
> The growing wheat, the growing weeds,
> The toiling horses, the tired men;
> The long empty roads,
> Sullen fires of sunset, fading,
> The eternal, unresponsive sky.
> Against all this, Youth,
> Flaming like the wild roses,
> Singing like the larks over the plowed fields,
> Flashing like a star out of the twilight;
> Youth with its insupportable sweetness,
> Its fierce necessity,
> Its sharp desire,
> Singing and singing,
> Out of the lips of silence,
> Out of the earthy dusk.[12]

In this poem, and in Cather's poetry and fiction in general, there is an element of the "mystical conception of the frontier" and of the "ultimate beneficence of . . . nature."[13] Nevertheless, "Prairie Spring" also casts doubt on the idea that nature is an ultimate good or a sacred garden. "Harshness," "weeds," "toil," and a blazing sun in an "unresponsive sky" make Cather homesick for the hills of Virginia, and these elements alien to paradise preview the redefinition of the sacred worldview that one finds in Willa Cather's novels.[14]

The sacred natural world, which describes America the garden, was characterized by a benevolent environment, a meeting place for humanity and the transcendent, and by human beings who occupy a central role in that environment and who are of supreme importance in the eyes of the supernatural. Willa Cather's fiction pictures a natural world that is different from the nature of the romantic poets and from the sacred conception of America (as outlined in chapter 1) in at least four ways. First, nature in Cather's fiction is *not* always the benevolent environment that a paradisiacal garden requires. Second, in Cather's natural world, human beings are peripheral—they are not the center of the universe, and it is the hostile natural world that is responsible for this peripheral existence on the frontier. This picture sharply contrasts to the romantic notion that human beings constitute a supreme position within a benevolent creation. Third, not only are characters peripheral in their world but marginal as well; they are of little significance, because they are not at home in their world but caught between two or more conflicting worlds. Finally, in the romantic world, nature is a receptacle for and a gateway to otherness. However, in Cather's fiction, the natural world of the prairie no longer functions as the sacred meeting ground for humankind and the divine. Rather, the natural world manifests itself as the object of the pioneer's struggle and, thus, as otherness itself.

The following pages explore the way that Cather's fiction redefines the romantic worldview in these four ways as it begins to paint a picture of a secularized American natural world—a natural world devoid of supernatural presence. Furthermore, it should be noted now that these same four reconstructive ideas, in Cather's revision of natural space, appear in Dreiser's fiction as applied to social space. Thus, where Cather's frontier is not always benevolent, neither is Dreiser's city; where Cather's pioneer is peripheral and marginal, so is Dreiser's urban dweller; where Cather's frontier loses its sacred quality and becomes otherness itself, so does Dreiser's social world.

The first characteristic of the natural environment in Cather's fiction appears in the form of the hostile world in *O Pioneers!* The land in this novel is both creative and destructive, beneficent and forbidding, as pioneers struggle against almost impossible odds in an untamed and "Wild Land." Thus, the land appears as sacred land, which manifests the awesome power of the supernatural, and it demonstrates a dark and powerful side as well as a benevolent side. In fact, the awesomeness of the land adds to its mysterious nature and lends the land a sense of otherness.[15] However, the concept of a hostile environment is not limited to the first section of *O Pioneers!* Rather, the theme of hostility of the land runs throughout Cather's work and occurs when the natural world contains elements that are antithetical to the purposes of the characters. The individual's struggle against the hostile setting to survive within it is a prominent theme throughout Cather's fiction.[16] Cather's picture of space is reminiscent of the nineteenth-century realists and describes a space where the characters fall victim to an antagonistic environment.

Cather's prairie novels best exemplify the antagonistic role of the physical environment in Cather's fiction. For example, *O Pioneers!* is the story of Alexandra Bergson's life on the American frontier and opens during Alexandra's childhood when the frontier is still "The Wild Land." This land is only for the hardiest of souls, and the settlers on the Nebraska prairie soon learn that few of them can survive on the frontier, because the frontier is the epitome of natural strength and is usually hostile. At the beginning of the book the land "was an enigma. It was like a horse that no one knows how to break to harness, that runs wild and kicks things to pieces."[17]

This frontier, which began as the "wild land" in *O Pioneers!*, represents an antagonistic force in the world. It is this hostile world that stands in the way of personal fulfillment, that the pioneers attempt to overcome, and that constitutes a testing ground that separates the fit from the unfit. Furthermore, in *My Ántonia*, the land is again very important in terms of representing an antagonistic force that impedes the freedom of human beings. Again, the harsh land dominates the world of the characters in the story, and this setting provides a test for those characters. As in *O Pioneers!*, only a few pass the test and are able to remain on the frontier. This fact is symbolized in an image that Jim, Ántonia, and the hired girls witness after a pleasure excursion into the natural world. As they watched the sun go down, and

> as the lower edge of the red disk rested on the high fields against the horizon, a great black figure suddenly appeared on the face of the sun. . . . In a moment we realized what it was. On some upland farm, a plough had been left standing in the field. The sun was sinking just behind it. Magnified across the distance by the horizontal light, it stood out against the sun, was exactly contained within the circle of the disk; the handles, the tongue, the share-black against the molten red. There it was, heroic in size, a picture writing on the sun[18]

The abandoned "plough" is highly symbolic. On the one hand, it appears to be suggesting that the pioneer is a hero and that his struggle is of the highest magnitude. Yet, on the other hand, the "plough" is a symbol of defeat and frustration and speaks of the abandoned fields. One more defeated farmer could not last in the harsh conditions that were cruel tests of fortitude. The test of the land is tough, and the attrition rate is high.

This concept of the antagonistic land strikes directly at the romantic conception of nature. The sacred world was benevolent and housed a good God; however, the pioneers in Cather's fiction could count on no such world. There is "no friendly god . . . hovering over them; . . . the universe in which they live is completely indifferent to them."[19] Therefore, the hostile nature of Cather's fictional world is the key to the secularized natural world that is the setting for her work. Furthermore, with the death of God in the natural world, the setting itself takes over a deterministic role. Determinism in Cather's work is rare, and it never develops into the full-blown determinism of the American naturalists; however, the setting does play a deterministic role in Cather's work as the characters fall prey to and are at the mercy of their own environments.[20]

The antagonistic environment of the frontier—the "bitter cold, scorching heat, and wind without rain — . . . unconsciously shaped and twisted the lives of the people."[21] This life for Cather's fictional pioneers is physically intolerable; however, nature also governs the emotional as well as the physical characteristics of life and affects the character's sense of "self-identity."[22] Thus, even the emotional state of Cather's characters seems to be intimately related to the physical environment they call home.

There is one very important emotional characteristic that develops in Cather's characters as a direct result of the hostile world of her setting. Not only does the lonely prairie isolate the pioneers physically from the rest of the world, but it also alienates them emotionally. The environment stifles, alienates, and imprisons most of Cather's characters because they are drawn toward it. This imprisoning nature of the land is usually negative and results in emotional depression.[23] Even Alexandra admits this stifling effect of the cruel land as she speaks to Carl, who did escape and move away from the harsh and relentless prairie.

I'd rather have had your freedom than my land. . . . We grow hard and heavy here. We don't move lightly and easily as you do, and our minds get stiff. If the world were no wider than my cornfields, if there were not something beside this, I wouldn't feel that it was much worth while to work. No, I would rather have Emil like you than like them. I felt that as soon as you came.[24]

Even though the theme of a constricting and isolating environment dominates Cather's prairie fiction, it also extends beyond prairie settings. For example, in *The Song of the Lark,* the setting is not the wild land but the small town. Moonstone provides the setting for Thea Kronberg, the daughter of a Methodist minister, to begin her rise to opera stardom. However, in order to obtain fame, Thea must first overcome obstacles and escape the constricting effects of her small-town environment—the limitations of Moonstone life that are graphically represented by Ray Kennedy and the railroad and that determine the life of the village.[25] The test for Thea is not the frontier as it is for the pioneers; however, the test is still the test that environment imposes upon a character—a test that threatens to crush the dreams of those who fail. Once again it is the setting that threatens to stifle the character and that represents a type of antagonistic force that must be overcome.

The same situation is present in the case of Claude Wheeler, the protagonist in *One of Ours.* Claude's environment—an established farm in Nebraska—is totally antithetical to Claude's aspirations and development. Claude wants to go to school and to widen the horizons of his world; however, events conspire to keep him chained to his stifling world on a Nebraska farm. Because of his narrow world, his tyrannical father, and his ineffectual mother, Claude's dreams remain unrealized; he marries the wrong girl; and his hopeless situation becomes even more unbearable.[26] For Claude, the impediment is a constricting environment and the release comes when he discovers a type of escape in World War I.

Claude experiences a rite of passage in his journey to the French battlefields as a flu epidemic breaks out on his ship. Many die from the epidemic, but Claude remains healthy, and he plays an important role in caring for the sick. After this ritual preparation, Claude eventually becomes a hero on a foreign battlefield and gives his life in the attempt to discover self-understanding. He finds what he could never find on his farm in Nebraska—he discovers fulfillment. Claude's story highlights the failure of the American dream concerning the West as the place of opportunity. Claude is crushed by the West and only encounters true opportunity for self-realization in an heroic effort in a foreign land. This contrasts to Cather's other works that are dominated by foreign immigrants who come to America in order to start a new life, and who often find only disappointment and death.

All of these examples have one characteristic in common.

There is some aspect of the environment of Cather's characters that is antagonistic to their needs and purposes and that usually provides some type of test for the characters. Whether or not they pass this test determines whether or not they experience self-actualization. In the beginning all of Cather's characters are peripheral, because their setting reduces their importance by imposing limitations upon them. If they pass the test that the setting presents them, then they regain centrality within their world. However, if they fail, like Dreiser's characters they remain imprisoned on the periphery of their hostile world. Thus, the second major theme in Cather's work as it redefines the romantic world-view is that human beings are peripheral in their world.

One major result of the Darwinian revolution was the removal of the human race from its central position in the cosmos. Cather's fiction emulates and encourages this shift by negating the romantic tendency to make characters central to the workings of their settings and by dislocating her characters on the indifferent and hostile frontier—the frontier itself is the great leveling agent of humanity. Whereas the romantic world and the American dream picture a physical country that affords opportunity of transcendence and betterment, Cather's setting works in the opposite manner and levels humanity to the same low and depressed state. Rather than being a place where everyone can succeed, the West for Cather is a place where only a few are able to climb from the loneliness and poverty of the periphery to the inclusive world of the center.

A significant passage from *My Ántonia* illustrates this reversal of the romantic view of space. In *My Ántonia,* a Russian immigrant, Peter, would like to see America as the place of opportunity. In his native Russia "only rich people [have] cows, but here any man could have one who would take care of her."[27] Thus, on the frontier, everyone starts on the same level, but this is as far as opportunity extends. The land offers opportunity, but the land is barren—it does not allow the realization of the dream that accompanies the promise of opportunity.[28] Very few ever realize success because they are limited to their depressed state and peripheral existence by an indifferent land that affords little access to the inner workings of their world.

On one level this indifferent frontier environment acts as a universal leveling agent of humanity, and because of this, the hostile world of the prairie pushes humanity from the center to the periphery. As a result, in Cather's fiction most of her characters are peripheral—they do not participate in the central workings of their world. However, Cather's characters suffer a third fate on the frontier, which is the universal leveling agent, that magnifies the insignificance of characters within their world. In addition to being peripheral, Cather's characters are marginal and insignificant parts of their setting because they are caught between two worlds (the worlds of opportunity and imprisonment; success and failure); they are dislocated and belong to no world. The most obvious example of this marginality comes with Cather's extensive characterization of immigrant families who dominate her novels (especially her prairie and frontier novels) and who are lost between two worlds. They try to continue the ways of the old world while attempting to exist in the new world, and as a result, they lose their identity and their sense of purpose.[29]

Nevertheless, one does not have to be an immigrant in a strange land to be marginal in Cather's fictional world. As mentioned earlier, Claude Wheeler is a marginal figure in his native Nebraska, for he is not at home even when he is in the house that he built for himself and Enid. Another marginal character in her own native land is Marian Forrester in *A Lost Lady,* who is condemned to a life in Sweet Water while she dreams of a more exciting life in more intriguing places. Her world is a stranger to her, and it serves to imprison her physically and spiritually. Mrs. Forrester's exclamation to Niel reveals her imprisonment and her need to escape the world where she is only a marginal character. "You see, two years, three years, more of this, and I could still go back to California—and live again. . . . That's what I'm struggling for, to get out of this hole. . . ."[30] Mrs. Forrester is trapped between two worlds—the world of Sweet Water and the more exciting world that she desires, and she is as much out of place with her environment as are the immigrant families in *O Pioneers!* and in *My Ántonia.*

Perhaps Cather's most disinherited and dislocated character is Father Latour in *Death Comes for the Archbishop.* As Latour nears his death, he contemplates returning to his native France to die after a life of missionary service in New Mexico. However, he had made a recent trip to his native land, and he was "homesick for the New" World while in the Old.[31] At the end of his life, Father Latour is at home neither in the Old World nor in the New; he is a stranger to New Mexico even after long years of traveling across the desert, yet he is even more a stranger to his native land, France. He has lost even the dream of a world where he can be a central figure.

Nevertheless, Cather's characters are not hopelessly embroiled in the confusion of the marginal situation, because some, like Latour and Claude, are able at least partially to overcome their dislocation—Claude becomes a hero and Latour builds his cathedral. In fact, many of Cather's characters hurdle their obstacles and overcome their insignificant position in the world where they find themselves through interaction with their setting. The very condition that produces the marginality in the first place also provides the means of escape; the setting, the environment, the characters' world makes it possible for the marginal characters to overcome their disinherited status and to thrust themselves into the mainstream of life. The setting is the great equalizer that not only handicaps everyone to the same degree but that also provides everyone with the same starting point and advantages. Thus, Cather's setting is not a deterministic or naturalistic environment that only places constraints upon characters but one that also provides them with opportunities.[32] This compromise of the determining ability of setting is a theme that I shall develop in part 4 of this chapter through an examination of Cather's redefinition of the Darwinian worldview.

Finally, Cather's fiction redefines the romantic, sacred worldview in a fourth way that develops out of the first three aspects of her redefinition. For the romantic poets, the natural world was a sacred garden because it disclosed the infinite; therefore, the object of the romantic's worship was the "other" that was beyond nature. In Cather's fiction there is no "other" beyond the natural world that can be experienced only through transcendence of the natural. Rather, Cather's setting itself embodies otherness. In Cather's fictional world, the environment—especially the frontier—presents itself as "other;" nature is massive and human beings are microcosmic, and the pioneers of these novels are involved in a struggle with and against a natural realm.[33] This struggle takes on spiritual and religious dimensions, for the object of the pioneers' piety is the physical, natural world that can crush, defeat, and yet give life to the weary pioneers who are practically helpless to its whims.

This last aspect of Cather's redefinition of the romantic worldview most dramatically demonstrates how her fiction participates in the secularization of American space. When the frontier embodies otherness itself, it loses its ability to disclose the transcendent (indeed it negates the need to disclose the transcendent), and, therefore, the land loses its sacred significance. When the natural world itself becomes ultimate, the secularization of that natural

environment has taken place, because the ultimate becomes familiar. As the pioneer approaches this secular land as "other," he or
she is overwhelmed by its awesome domination of life. This awe
is what creates the pioneer spirit—the need to conquer nature
rather than to commune with and transcend nature (as the romantic poets did). And it is the pioneer's driving need to overcome nature—to reduce otherness—that destroys the sacred
character of the land, that secularizes American natural space,
and that leads to the decline of the noble pioneer and the awesome frontier. This rebellion against the otherness of the land
through Cather's story chronicles the demise of the noble West
and secularizes natural America in three stages. First, the taming
of the frontier destroys its sacred and awe-inspiring nature; second, modern civilization taints the pristine West further; and finally, materialistic intrusions into the West destroy the pioneer's
nobility forever.

The first step in this denial of the otherness of the land develops from the destruction of the mysterious and awesome nature
of the land. This destruction is usually depicted as the noble ac-
complishment of the pioneer hero, and many of Cather's critics
err in characterizing her as the romantic and wistful champion
of this noble frontiersman.[34] Cather's pioneers do seem noble at
times, and they are certainly to be admired more than their city
counterparts. Nevertheless, a close reading of the corpus of Cather's works reveals a less than idealistic picture of the pioneering
hero or heroine. In fact, instead of perpetuating the frontier
myth, as James Fenimore Cooper's frontier does, Cather's fiction
dispels it through her presentation of the fall of the heroic pioneer.[35] The pioneer's failure is not, finally, the result of weak wills
or a dominating environment but the result of an improper approach toward the world. The failure of the pioneer finds deep
roots in the American dream of sacred possibility concerning
western land—a vision that drew pioneers west in search of an
agrarian American dream of possibility and prosperity through
taming the frontier. It is this urge to "master their environment"[36]
that leads to the pioneers' hostile relationship with the western
land and to their ultimate defeat at the mercy of an uncaring wilderness.

Thus, the taming of the wild land in Cather's novels is the first
step toward the American's secularization of natural space.[37] "The
Wild Land," as it appears in the first section of O Pioneers!, has
a sacred quality—it is awesome and awe-inspiring. The "endless
prairie, freed of physical limitations," liberates the spirits of the

pioneers who experience it in that way. This wild prairie possesses a type of sacred order that reflects the power and purpose of God—a type of sacred order that makes it like an unspoiled Eden.[38] Yet, this sacred quality of the land is lost in Cather's fiction. The sacred natural world cannot retain its character against the onslaught of the western-moving pioneers and fortune seekers. The very act of taming the wildness, of controlling the otherness, spoils the sacredness of the land as the pioneers master the harsh environment and make it "bear harvests."[39] Thus, although the later introduction of modern civilization and materialism to the frontier is much more damaging than the poor yeoman farmer, the pioneer still represents the first step in the secularization of American natural space. The pioneer destroys the "other" quality within the land by humanizing it, taming it, and by attempting to make it conform to human need and desire.

The second stage of the secularization of natural space in Cather's fiction follows closely on the heels of the first and appears as the intrusion of modern civilization on the frontier. There is a tendency in Cather's stories that equates progress and modernity with "loss of meaning . . . [in] the primary areas of human experience" and with moral and intellectual bankruptcy.[40] This notion is the main theme in *A Lost Lady*—a novel that tells the story of the decline of the last of the true pioneers (Captain Forrester) and the rise to importance of men compelled by progress (Ivy Peters). Those characters who have no allegiance to the frontier (Marian Forrester) are far removed from the "spirit of the land" and fall victim to the modern advance of scoundrels like Ivy Peters.[41] As the primacy of the land declines in the hearts of the pioneers, the need to change the West into a picture of modern civilization and progress grows stronger. This transition occurs in Cather's fiction and appears reprehensible.

This dreaded modern civilization occurs often in the guise of the village or the city and the railroad that makes the town possible. In *My Ántonia,* a transition in setting occurs that produces a prejudice against the town and modernizing machines such as the railroad. The land of Ántonia's childhood appears as a sacred and awe-inspiring garden—an Eden of sorts. Yet, in the second section of the novel, the town emerges on the scene as a restrictive and domineering environment for Ántonia—one in which restrictive convention denies the desire to live fully and happily. Later, Ántonia elopes with a railroad man to the city only to be abandoned and shamed. Her only peace comes when she returns to the land, marries a farmer, and regains that wholesome existence she knew as a child. In her rebirth, she becomes an earth goddess and is redeemed by her return to and appreciation of the land she once knew.[42]

Perhaps the best example of the supremacy of country life to city life occurs in "Neighbour Rosicky" as Rosicky compares the virtues of country life to city slums.

> In the country, if you had a mean neighbour, you could keep off his land and make him keep off yours. But in the city, all the foulness and misery and brutality of your neighbours was part of your life. The worst things he had come upon in his journey through the world were human,—depraved and poisonous specimens of man. To this day he could recall certain terrible faces in the London streets. There were mean people everywhere, to be sure, even in their own country town here. But they weren't tempered, hardened, sharpened, like the treacherous people in cities who live by grinding or cheating or poisoning their fellow-men. He had helped to bury two of his fellow-workmen in the tailoring trade, and he was distrustful of the organized industries that see one out of the world in big cities. Here, if you were sick, you had Doctor Ed to look after you; and if you died, fat Mr. Haycock, the kindest man in the world, buried you.
>
> It seemed to Rosicky that for good, honest boys like his, the worst they could do on the farm was better than the best they would be likely to do in the city.[43]

This disdain for modern civilization continues in a negative way as the industrial or scientific world is pictured as that which impinges upon natural sacral order. For example, in *Alexander's Bridge*, Cather deals with the industrial, engineering society. The story describes the collapse of a bridge and, thus, the failure of the modern society that had the technical ability to build it. Furthermore, science is directly attacked in *The Professor's House*, because it indiscriminantly pursues progress and advancement at the expense of the otherness of life. Professor St. Peter launches into an extemporaneous speech during one of his seminars and attacks the evils of the scientific world.

> Science hasn't given us any new amazements. . . . It hasn't given us any richer pleasures, . . . nor any new sins—not one! Indeed, it takes our old ones away. . . . [It takes away the human ability of] believing in the mystery and importance of their own little individual lives.[44]

Science, technological knowledge, and industrial progress destroy the sense of "other" that the American natural world once commanded. Science takes away the sense of mystery and the sense of sacredness in the world, and it leaves humanity abandoned in an uncaring, hostile, and secular universe.

The third intrusion into the natural world, which taints sacred America and leads to its secularization and to the pioneers' defeat, is the materialism that results from the advent of modern civilization and its greed. Materialism accompanies the pioneer's free-enterprising spirit and the baron's industrializing tendencies, and its spoils the sacred nature of natural space once and for all. Once the noble pioneer loses sight of the struggle with a sacred force (the frontier) and turns his sights to the materialistic gain to be wrought from humanizing the land, he forfeits his noble image of one close to nature and, thus, to God. Then the land gives itself over to "petty men, unrestrained greed, and dangerous popular demands, . . . [and the] exploitation of nature . . . [by] petty materialists" replaces the admiration of nature by the noble frontiersman.[45]

It is at this point that critical confusion concerning Cather's conception of the pioneering farmer reigns. Critics have a difficult time reconciling Cather's view of the pioneer as sometimes noble and sometimes reprehensible. But this confusion exists only if one reads Cather's fiction as if character development is the dominating artistic concern. Cather writes not so much about the intrinsic qualities of the pioneers as she does about their struggle with their environment and about their approach to existence within that environment. In Cather's fiction, the pioneer loses nobility only when he or she approaches the natural world as a means to success rather than as an awesome natural force—rather than as a sacred avenue to otherness. When "a farmer exchanges things with an intrinsic value (wheat, corn, cattle) for 'manufactured articles . . . [and] machinery,'" then he or she has lost a sense of closeness with the land and exchanged it for material success.[46] This intrusion of materialistic success destroys the sacred character of the natural world for the pioneer, and it directly leads to the decline of the West and to the secularization of natural space in Cather's works.

Thus, in Cather's fiction, the pioneer does not destroy the pristine glory of the frontier as long as he or she lives in harmony with nature. In fact, farming itself does not change the sacred aura and mystery of the land as long as farming does not become an enterprise that subjects the shape and intent of the landscape to commercial interests. The problem of commercial farming is that nature becomes a means toward an end and not an end or value in itself. Commercial farming is oriented by the goals of progress, success, and control of the frontier and eventually leads to the despoliation of a pristine frontier.[47] The destruction of the glory of the frontier in Cather's fiction is recounted in a similar fashion by Howard Mumford Jones.

> In sum, . . . the lost glory of the agrarian frontier cannot be recovered, or at least cannot be recovered so long as the nation is dedicated to a materialistic culture, the worship of the bitch goddess, Success.[48]

This theme of an intruding materialistic culture occurs throughout Cather's work. For example, in *My Ántonia*, the town environment is decadent while the unspoiled frontier is described in noble terms. In *The Professor's House*, the commercialization of Tom Outland's invention threatens the noble memory that Professor St. Peter holds of Tom. This is significant because Tom is one of the few Cather characters who discovers how to live harmoniously in a sacred and unspoiled natural environment. In *One of Ours*, the Wheeler farm is the epitome of the commercial farming venture, and as a result, it is also a stifling and crippling environment for Claude. Yet, the best example of the secularization of natural space as a result of the intrusion of materialism appears in *A Lost Lady*. Captain Forrester, the last vestige of a noble and dying pioneer race, succumbs to the likes of Ivy Peters, the decadent representative of a new race of men who are intent upon materializing the frontier. Thus, with a symbolic defeat of the frontier spirit, Ivy drains the marsh, which Captain Forrester refused to disturb, in order to plant cash crops "with an air of proprietorship."[49] *A Lost Lady* chronicles the final capitulation of the sacred frontier to an encroaching march of despicable materialists.

Cather's fiction redefines the romantic, sacred view of American natural space with the following four assertions: (1) nature is not always benevolent; (2) human beings are no longer central in their world but are peripheral creatures at best; (3) characters are not at home in their world but are caught between two worlds—they are marginal; (4) the land itself loses its ability to disclose otherness and instead takes upon itself a sense of mystery, power, and otherness, which can (indeed should) create respect and awe in response. A secularization of the American frontier in Cather's novels comes about through the attempt to tame the land, through the encroachment of modern civilization, and through the commercialization of the land. In short, secularization of American natural space occurs when characters attempt to reduce the otherness of nature and to control the natural world.

The American dream of opportunity is thus an ambivalent one—one that offers success only at the price of that which makes success possible. Thus, the pioneer suffers defeat—Anton Shimerda commits suicide; Captain Forrester dies a shell of a man; Alexandra experiences tragedy and the inability to love anything except the land; and Claude must flee the successful frontier in search of new frontiers of possibility. In the end it is clear that the American dream of the frontier (success and opportunity) is a questionable and inadequate vision that destroys the very character of the land that offers the dream. In Cather's fiction, "the struggle rather than the prize is admirable;"[50] the means, that is, legitimate the end; the conquest of the land replaces harmony with and respect of the natural world.

4. Willa Cather's Fiction and the Redefinition of Natural Space in Response to Darwinism

Cather's redefinition of the romantic vision of sacred space is accompanied by the intrusion of determinism into her fictional world. Indeed, one might expect a developed naturalism to be Cather's response to the sacred American garden. Cather's settings tend to dominate and determine the lives of individuals; however, her deterministic tendency is not simple determinism in the Darwinian or Spencerian mode. Cather is not a naturalist who describes a world where individuals are helpless to the whims of an uncaring natural world. Thus, in her fiction Cather redefines natural space by redefining the Darwinian conception of the natural world as well as the sacred conception of the world. Once again, it is at this point that parallels to Dreiser's fiction become obvious, for Dreiser, too, struggled with sacred and naturalistic constructions of the world. In Cather's case, simple natural selection and survival of the fittest are not sufficient to completely explain the intricacies of the physical world and of the human place in that world. Instead, in Cather's redefined world, harmony does not exist in the natural world alone but requires a proper response by human beings to the natural world and to one another. Thus, in response to a Darwinian, uncaring world, Cather constructs a setting where relationships to the environment and to one another are primary—a setting balanced by the partial recovery of that *lost* world of sacred significance.

Cather's characters are ultimately determined neither by Darwinian survival of the fittest nor by random variation and natural selection. Alexandra Bergson survives and succeeds not because of any great physical strength but because she possesses a moral determination to dedicate herself to the land. Furthermore, the Darwinian concept of natural selection fails in Cather's fiction as well as that of survival of the fittest. Marian Forrester suffers in spite of her great beauty and physical superiority, which are not enough to keep her from missing out on happiness. Mrs. Forrester fails in spite of her natural endowments because she does not possess the moral strength that Alexandra obtains by the end of *O Pioneers!* Marian Forrester compromises herself to Ivy Peters, and in doing so she destroys any advantage nature may have given her through her absence of the moral sense to establish a proper human relationship. Likewise, natural talent is not enough to insure Thea Kronberg her success as a singer. Rather, it is Thea's virtuous character that sets her apart from the others. In every case, the moral insight of the individual transcends the constraints and advantages that environment places upon the individual, and Darwinian determinism is not applicable.

Thus, physical superiority in the natural world is not sufficient to guarantee success in Cather's fictional world—conquering the elements does not make the pioneer a fulfilled individual. Rarely, in Cather's work, does a character experience harmony in the natural world as one might expect, if the natural world is governed by Darwin's rules. However, this is because the pioneers do not approach the natural world properly, and they abuse and misuse the frontier for their own personal gain. But there is an element of harmony in Cather's novels, and this element always appears in the natural world *before* the frontiersman is able to humanize the environment and secularize the sacred, unspoiled land. Thus, a harmonious existence in the natural world is directly dependent on the amount of secularizing influence human beings have exerted upon the land.

By painting the Darwinian world as insufficient, and by seeking to recover the harmony of the virgin West, Cather's fiction redefines a world that depends on something other than physical laws to create order. That "something other" occurs in Cather's fiction in the environment that retains its sacred significance—in the setting that exists *before* the western settlers secularize it. In other

words, even though Cather recognizes and chronicles the secularization of American natural space, she is never wholly comfortable with secularity because of its tendency toward deperson-
alization. This "something other" is most obviously depicted in ancient Indian societies and in their attitudes toward the desert
Southwest. An examination of these settings in Cather's fiction
clarifies her opposition to secularization and modernization, and
it illustrates her ambivalence to a world conception that operates
according to physical law.

The majority of Cather's settings occur on the frontier that is
in the process of decline or that has already succumbed to the secularizing influences of modernization. Such modernization comes
at the hands of eager pioneers who want to dominate the land
by conquering it and, thus, by denying its otherness. However,
from time to time, Cather's reader encounters an environment
that has not been humanized—an environment that still maintains sacred qualities. The primordial land is a favorite image for
Cather, and these images are key to her fiction.[51] For it is the ancient land, the land of the Indian Cliff Dwellers, that maintains
mystical and mysterious forces in the natural world and, thus, sacred significance. The experience of this land is beyond the grasp
of the majority of Cather's characters, but its distant presence continues to haunt these characters.

This harmonious land of the ancient tribes is sacred, and the
pioneering secularization of the frontier is the first step toward
destroying the sacred significance of the land. In Cather's fiction,
"the ethically best man is he who lives closest to nature."[52] Likewise, the ethically despicable person is one who neither cares for
nor respects the natural world. These two ethical stances to the
natural world set up a hierarchy of relationship between environment and character in Cather's fiction. Cather's starting point is
the sacred, unspoiled prairie. Most of her characters do not recognize the sacrality of this virgin land and approach the land as
something to be dominated. The consequences for these characters manifest themselves through antagonistic and improper relationships with the land and with other characters. However,
Cather's enlightened characters recognize the sacredness, the otherness, of the land and are able to maintain proper relationships
with the land and with other people. It is crucial to note that, for
Cather, personal fulfillment and harmony depend upon relating
successfully to both the natural world and to other people. The
interconnectedness of social and natural relationships constitutes
Dreiser's secularizing theme as well, yet he arrives here by pictur-

ing the secularization of the social world while Cather begins with the natural environment.

Cather's enlightened characters who can live harmoniously in the natural and social environment are represented most often by the ancient Indian tribes. Nevertheless, some modern characters in Cather's fiction also participate in this reciprocal relationship with the natural environment. These characters must undergo some rite of passage before they can approach the world without the exploitative eyes of their companions. For example, before Tom Outland can penetrate the mysteries of the Cliff Dwellers, he must first cross a river that no one has crossed before. Similarly, before Claude Wheeler can tackle new frontiers and escape the confining West of his youth, he must first cross the Atlantic Ocean and survive a severe flu epidemic. These rites of passage are rare and prepare one to experience the mystery of the land that the pioneers so quickly forget and fail to realize. Unlike Tom Outland, the pioneers do not acknowledge the otherness of the prairie, and their soiled spades penetrate and spoil the untried land. They do not realize that their spades need not be soiled, for they forget the secret of the ancient tribes who lived in harmony and in awe of the sacred landscape.

The distinguishing mark of these ancient societies is that they manage to live in harmony with the world around them in such a way that the physical environment retains its pristine and sacred character. This is in stark contrast to the advancing pioneers who tend to dominate and master the land in such a way that secularizes the natural world. The narratives describing the Indian's relationship to the land are always couched within a larger narrative and tend to constitute the means of self-discovery for one of the characters. As a result, Cather's picture of the ancient societies is not simply a romantic view of primitive cultures (like one might find in Cooper's fiction); rather, it is paradigmatic, and it extends beyond time and place to highlight the reason for the pioneer's failure.

Death Comes For the Archbishop is one of Cather's most critically acclaimed novels and is representative of her use of ancient societies to describe heightened approaches to living in the world. In this book, nature takes on a most obvious sacral quality as ancient Indian religion plays an important role to reinforce the nature of the land as sacred space. The Indians in New Mexico care only to preserve their land that is indispensible to the practice of their religion and to their very existence. "Their country . . . was a part of their religion; the two were inseparable. . . . their gods dwelt there."[53] Thus, the Indians, in *Death Comes For the Archbishop*, respect the sacred nature of the land and live harmoniously with it instead of trying to usurp the otherness of the land as do the pioneers.

But what does this harmonious existence entail? This harmony involves the Indians' innate sense of oneness with nature—a sense of oneness that allows the Indians to accommodate themselves to nature rather than attempting to accommodate nature to their own selfish desires. The Indians do not try to master or violate a natural world that is sacred but learn to live in harmony and peace with nature, using nature to satisfy only the most basic survival needs.[54] Thus, Cather's fiction contrasts the Indians' approach to the natural world to the white man's approach. The Indians accommodate themselves to the natural world because they are awed by its sacred quality while the pioneering settlers seek to master and control the natural world in their search for prosperity. The native lands for the Indians are "places more sacred to them than churches, more sacred than any place is to the white man."[55]

However, the Indian does not approach the land differently because he or she is an Indian. Others can see and appropriate the natural world in sacred terms as well. What is important is not the otherness of race, but the awed stance toward environment. The Mexicans in *Death Comes For the Archbishop* are similar to the Indians in their approach to the physical world, and they recognize the sacredness of the natural realm and seek to preserve that quality of their world. Thus, they do not desecrate the land for commercial or even for survival purposes. Rather, even their adobe dwellings utilize natural materials from the earth and stand in quiet harmony with the surrounding countryside.[56]

Although the white race can only approximate the Indian and Mexican ideal of recognizing and respecting the sacred character of nature, on rare occasions someone gains this insight. Father Latour, the missionary priest in *Death Comes For the Archbishop*, comes close to recognizing the sacred quality of the natural world. In his travels throughout the wild country of New Mexico during the latter half of the nineteenth century, he often associates the land and nature with his religious beliefs and with religious symbols. For example, a juniper tree reminds him of a crucifix and provides an appropriate chapel in the desert where he can pray. Later an Indian cave serves as a Gothic chapel for Latour, and an outcropping rock signifies to him the relationship of Christ and Peter. Throughout the novel, events and forms in the natural surroundings remind Latour of his own religious heritage, symbolize "religious realities . . . [and] 'holy mysteries'," and allow Latour access to "'the one supreme spiritual experience.'"[57] This spiritual experience of the sacred natural world is symbolized by the cathedral he builds from the native stone of the region. This is his statement on the harmonious existence that one should seek with one's surroundings.

Besides Latour, a few other enlightened characters in Cather's fiction recognize that the proper way to exist in one's environment should come through respect and harmony rather than through domination. This is Alexandra's insight in *O Pioneers!* when she recognizes that the wild land is superior to the settled land.[58] However, she does not make this recognition until after she spends her life in the effort to dominate and tame the land. Another character in *O Pioneers!*, Crazy Ivar, intuits the proper, harmonious relationship one should have with nature and appears as a stark contrast with Alexandra who is the supreme defiler of nature.[59] As a result, Crazy Ivar, who participates in the sacred character of the land, is the one character who is close enough to the sacred reality of the land to announce the sin of Marie and Emil near the end of the novel.[60] Ivar's judgment is aimed at those who do not establish harmony with their world—the sin is failing to respect the integrity of the natural and virginal land.

Perhaps the character who best describes the harmonious relationship one should preserve with nature is Jim Burden. Jim's description of the prairie in *My Ántonia* hints at the sacredness of the natural world. "The whole prairie was like the bush that burned with fire and was not consumed."[61] This clear reference to the burning bush of Moses implies that the prairie is holy ground that should not be tread upon and made unclean. Jim's description of the prairie is a description of the land that had not yet been plowed under and farmed—it was the land untarnished by the pioneers' humanizing tools. This is the land that is sacred in Cather's fiction, and this is the land with which one should endeavor to live harmoniously.

But even though most of the settings in Cather's work do not measure up to this glorious ideal, there is an underlying respect for the sacred quality of nature throughout her novels. For example, Ántonia turns back to the land for her salvation after losing herself in towns and cities. Her move to Black Hawk signals the fall of Ántonia, she meets Larry Donovan in the town, and she goes to Denver to marry him. The Denver experience is devastating for Ántonia, and she returns to Black Hawk unmarried and pregnant. Yet, by the end of the novel, Ántonia is cleansed of her experience in the city, returns to the land, experiences a rebirth of sorts, and takes on the stature of an "earth-goddess." The city is the setting where Ántonia finds only corruption while the *unspoiled* land maintains its purity and ability to provide freedom.[62] Nevertheless, this freedom is realizable only if one lives in harmony with the natural world—then and only then can the land be considered sacred.

Yet, for this natural world to be sacred requires more than just a harmonious existence with the natural itself. It requires a social and communal harmony as well—one that becomes clear once again with Cather's Indians, the Cliff Dwellers. Cather was awed by the Grand Canyon and the cliff dwellings that she visited during an Arizona vacation. The Canyon seemed pristine and natural to her, and the dwellings evoked mystical images for her fiction.[63] These cliff dwellings occur most importantly in *The Song of the Lark, The Professor's House,* and "The Enchanted Bluff" as spots beyond time and place—as the paradigm for harmonious existence with the natural and social worlds. Judith Fryer refers to these dwellings as felicitous space—space that helps define one's being.[64] As characters in Cather's works discover these dwellings, they begin to define or redefine their own being in light of their discovery of the ideal existence of those ancient Indians who lived there. These dwellings, like the land itself, are "a catalyst to a heightened consciousness and selfhood,"[65] and are paradigmatic for Cather's characters.

The two principal characters who encounter the cliff dwellings in a meaningful way are Tom Outland in *The Professor's House* and Thea Kronberg in *The Song of the Lark.* Their "vague mystic experience" is a result of the sacred nature of the Cliff City. They had never before encountered the "order wrought by man out of raw nature for his use and enjoyment—an orderliness that does not *destroy* nature but one which *builds* on primeval order."[66] Most critics deal with both of these encounters with the cliff dwellings in terms of the past and time;[67] however, setting is at least equally important when dealing with these cities. The Cliff City is, for Cather, the paradigm for an organization of natural space that does not spoil the sacred order inherent to that natural world; therefore, the cliff dwelling societies represent the type of setting that epitomizes sacred space and the effect that such a harmonious world exerts upon its human inhabitants.

This last suggestion concerning the affect of setting on character occurs in *The Song of the Lark* where the Southwest and the cliff dwellings have a direct influence upon Thea Kronberg, the protagonist of the novel. During Thea's rise to stardom, she vacations in Arizona for a summer at Panther Canyon—a summer that is the climatic point in Thea's personal development. As Thea experiences a critical point in her maturation as an artist, she finds herself awed by the beauty of the cliff dwellings in the canyon.[68] Inspired by the mystical beauty of the natural world, Thea is able to participate in the aesthetic and sacred quality of the landscape in a way that influences her own growth as an artist. The sacred land, the setting, of the Cliff Dwellers reaches beyond time and affects Thea spatially in a meaningful and life-changing way, as her reverence for natural order leads to personal and aesthetic maturity and allows her rise to stardom.

Nevertheless, the best example of Cather's use of the cliff dwellings occurs with Tom Outland's narrative in *The Professor's House*. In particular, the cliff dwellings are important to the story of Tom's summer in the Southwest on the mesa "in spiritual kinship with its former inhabitants, curiously dissociated from the rest of the world."[69] There are two narratives that parallel each other in this novel. The one tells of Tom's adventure in the Southwest, and the other recounts Professor St. Peter's longing for such adventure while wasting away in his own "spiritual Waste Land."[70] Tom's story describes the recovery of a sacred approach to natural space, while the Professor's story highlights the empty life that characterizes his existence in a secularized, secondhand view of the land that Tom experiences in his adventure. As concerns the natural world, the novel recounts the difference between the sacred land that Tom discovers and the secularized world that the Professor inhabits—between a meaningful and harmonious existence and an empty and shallow life.

Professor St. Peter suffers the inability to relate successfully either to the natural world or to those around him, and as a result, spends his energy in the attempt to transcend his dull life through a multivolumed history of Spanish explorers. Professor St. Peter never learns the key to meaningful, proper relationships, and he turns to experience beyond reality in order to satisfy his yearnings for meaning. For example, in the last chapters, St. Peter's suicidal mood and passive acceptance of possible death affirm that, for him, meaning and otherness lie beyond the world. Father Latour exhibits a similar acceptance of death, and both examples illustrate Cather's difficulty with the Darwinian worldview. Her fear is that Darwinian naturalism will remove otherness from the world, rather than ground otherness in the world, and will, thus, create dissatisfaction with reality. To combat such an attitude, Cather affirms something quite different in her redefinition of sacred land and the Darwinian world. For Cather, secularity, unlike naturalism, does not destroy otherness but locates it in the world. The proper approach to one's environment, then, must be one in which the affirmation of otherness is grounded—one which Tom's life on the mesa exemplifies through his discovery of the sacred qualities of nature.

For Tom, the "mesa was no longer an adventure, but a religious emotion," because the Cliff City was "a religious sanctuary."[71] The Cliff City is a religious sanctuary because the past inhabitants of the community, an ancient Indian tribe, recognized and preserved the sacred character of the land. They neither capitulated to the awesome power of nature because of a hopeless struggle with it (like John Bergson and Anton Shimerda) nor dominated the land and stripped it of its grandeur and mystical power (like Alexandra). Rather, the ancient Indians of the Cliff City recognized the unspoiled beauty of the land and learned to live harmoniously with it. Father Duchene comments on the sacred nature of the city as he describes the ancient struggle that produced such a harmonious order.

> Like you, I feel a reverence for this place. Wherever humanity has made that hardest of all starts and lifted itself out of mere brutality, is a sacred spot. Your people were cut off here without the influence of example or emulation, with no incentive but some natural yearning for order and security. The built themselves into this mesa and humanized it.[72]

However, the Cliff Dwellers humanized their environment in a much different way from the pioneers who settled the west. The Cliff Dwellers preserved the natural integrity of the land and lived in harmony with it, while the pioneers changed the face of the land and commercialized it. These two approaches to the natural world are key in Cather's fiction and highlight the secularizing tendency that Cather describes in her fiction.

Thus, Tom's Eden, complete with a decayed body that he named "Mother Eve," is sacred ground not because it is ancient but because it is unspoiled and exhibits ultimate order—an order that creates "a vision of the Heavenly City set in an aura of gold."[73] It is this order created by human beings in harmony with nature that creates and maintains the sacred character of the setting; yet, it is this order of harmony that is missing in the settled land of the pioneer's West. When the pioneers struggle against the land and lose, nature dominates human beings and destroys them. When the pioneers manage to impose their will upon the land and dominate it, then nature loses its sacred quality and is secularized. Both models appear in Cather's fiction about the frontier, and both models are models of disorder where human beings and nature are out of harmony. The harmonious example of Tom's Cliff City highlights the destructive effects that secularization of natural space can have to both the land and to human beings. It strengthens the call that the untamed and sacred wilderness exerts upon St. Peter and upon all who are sensitive to the land in its natural state.

> But if he [Professor St. Peter] went anywhere next summer, he thought it would be down into Outland's country, to watch the sunrise break on sculptured peaks and impassable mountain passes—to look off at those long, rugged, untamed vistas dear to the American heart. Dear to all hearts, probably—at least calling to all.[74]

Nevertheless, the Cliff City is sacred for a reason other than the harmonious existence with nature that the ancient Indians enjoyed. A sacred setting must involve "a strongly developed community sense in a close-to-nature setting," and this community sense occurs in the communal setting of the Cliff City. The implication in Cather's fiction is that one can develop proper personal relationships only if one can also maintain a proper relationship to the environment and vice versa. In other words, a harmonious existence depends upon striking a balanced harmony with one's world and with the people of that world. Even Tom Outland could not experience fully the meaning of the Cliff City because of his ruptured relationship with his companion Roddy Blake. The Cliff Dwellers created an ordered society with the natural and social world, yet for Tom, and for the majority of Cather's characters, this ordered harmony between nature and humanity never quite materializes.[75] This interconnection between relationships and one's approach to the natural is perhaps the most important one in Cather's fiction, and it highlights the difference between meaning and frustration in this world.

I must sum up Cather's redefinition of Darwin's worldview before continuing. First, Cather rejects a purely deterministic world where human beings are only products of their environments. It follows that natural selection and survival of the fittest do not operate as strict laws in the human world. Third, harmony does not exist in the natural world alone; rather, for harmony to exist requires the proper response by human beings to the natural world. Finally, human relationships are important, and perhaps key, in the fiction of Willa Cather. In a Darwinian world, relationships never rise above the physical struggle to survive, but Cather strikes a blow at the Darwinian isolation of physical laws and struggles as she reinstates the importance of proper moral and spiritual relationships.

5. Human Relationships in Cather's Fiction and Rebellion Against a Darwinian World

Inadequate and broken human relationships dominate Cather's fiction. In the prairie novels, humanizing and conquering the land (secularizing space) replaces meaningful human relationships so that the quest for opportunity and success dominates life to such a great extent that human relationships become secondary. In fact, human relationships tend to get in the way of success—"love and compassion [are] a hindrance to self-realization,"[76] and relationships are perceived as a hindrance to material success rather than as a form of human fulfillment. However, human relationships are, in Cather's fiction as in Dreiser's, absolutely necessary for a fulfilled and meaningful existence, and the failure of human relationships in Cather's fiction lends her work a sense of hopelessness.[77] Even though the pioneers might master nature and forge success from the wild land, they usually do so with the sacrifice of that which makes life meaningful—proper human relationships. This appears most clearly in *O Pioneers!* through the character of Alexandra Bergson.

Alexandra is strong-willed, and through sheer determination and sacrifice, she manages to tame the wild land of the prairie and to build a successful farm. She devotes herself totally to the land in order that Emil, her younger brother, will have a chance to go to college and escape the confines of the frontier life. Yet, this all-encompassing orientation to the land is not healthy or proper because Alexandra sacrifices her own identity to the goal of taming and subduing the land. This loss of self to the land is tragic because she also loses her chance at meaningful human relationships; she cannot "live fully and humanly," because to do so "requires exposure to the gamut of human experience. . . ."[78] Alexandra has no such exposure because she throws herself completely into her beloved land. Through her devotion to the land,

Alexandra humanizes it; however, in doing so, she is so indifferent to human passion and feeling that she fails to recognize the development of a tragic relationship between her best friend and Emil. Marie's and Emil's passion for one another is alien to Alexandra, and she does not realize their folly until death ends the illicit relationship.[79]

That Alexandra substitutes her dedication to the land for human relationships makes her relationships unnatural and less than satisfying. This appears clearly in passages that speak of her relationship to the land in sexual terms. She passes up a relationship with Carl Linstrum until the end of the novel, and then their friendship is little more than platonic. But throughout the novel, Alexandra replaces the lack of intimacy in her life with an erotic conception of the land she loves, and she gives herself to the land and becomes its lover.[80] The intimacy that exists between Alexandra and the land appears most clearly in Alexandra's recurring erotic dream. In this dream, Alexandra experiences

> an illusion of being lifted up bodily and carried lightly by some one very strong. It was a man, certainly, who carried her, but he was like no man she knew; he was much larger and stronger and swifter, and he carried her as easily as if she were a sheaf of wheat. She never saw him, but, with eyes closed, she could feel that he was yellow like the sunlight, and there was the smell of ripe cornfields about him. She could feel him approach, bend over her and lift her, and then she could feel herself being carried swiftly off across the fields.[81]

This subconscious relationship frustrates Alexandra, and perhaps makes her feel guilty, for after such a dream she would rise angrily and "prosecute her bath with vigor, finishing it by pouring buckets of cold well-water over her gleaming white body."[82] Cather's personification of the land demonstrates Alexandra's struggle with sexual feelings, and her denial of her sexuality lasts until the end of the novel when tragedy initiates a desire for a relationship with Carl.

Alexandra finds security in her love of the land and only risk in love for people. The relationship between Emil and Marie Shabata, which ends in tragedy and death, seems to support this suspicion of intense human relationships. Nevertheless, even though Marie and Emil die in each other's arms by Marie's jealous husband, Marie is a more admirable character than Alexandra, because Marie is able to love passionately while Alexandra can only express her feelings for the land. "There is a grandeur about Alexandra, but there is not warmth, . . . and even her indomitable energy seems cold beside Marie's tragic intensity."[83] Yet, one must not ignore Cather's insistence that the lovers were involved in an improper relationship as well, for their dishonest courtship carries consequences as does Alexandra's unnatural one.

The scene at the very beginning of the novel, when the seven-year-old (but even then seductive) Marie gives candy to the five-year-old Emil, foreshadows the relationship between Emil and Marie that comes to fruition years later.[84] It is this innocent childhood friendship that grows in adulthood into the "sin" that Crazy Ivar announces in his exclamation to Alexandra after finding the dead lovers. "'Mistress, mistress,' he sobs, 'it has fallen! Sin and death for the young ones! God have mercy upon us!'"[85] Crazy Ivar describes the *fall* of the garden motif. The lovers die under a white mulberry tree, and with their death the harmony of the garden vanishes.

Because of an illicit relationship, harmony with the natural world becomes impossible, the paradisiacal garden appears tarnished, and Alexandra's illusions concerning the sufficiency of the land break down. Emil and Marie find no harmony with the natural world, and the result is a tragic end to an improper relationship. Emil and Marie fall victim to the internal forces of nature—the sexual drive—because Marie is already a part of a failed human relationship with her husband Frank. The entire tragic drama revolves around the inability to enter into and maintain proper relationships with people and harmonious relationships with natural forces. Thus, in Cather's fiction, secularization affects social space as well as natural space. This reiterates the interconnectedness of the two realms and the similarity Cather's work holds to Dreiser's.

O Pioneers! is not the only one of Cather's stories to involve the theme of failed relationships. Marian Forrester in *A Lost Lady,* has difficulty holding onto a lasting relationship; Ántonia's first marriage ends in abandonment; Professor St. Peter finds that his marriage is but a shell of a relationship after descending from his retreat in his upstairs office; in *Lucy Gayheart,* Lucy has no meaningful relationship with her environment or with anyone around her, and her life is depressingly bare; *Sapphira and the Slave Girl* is based on a "moral wrong"—the moral wrong of slavery, and slavery is nothing but the institutionalization of improper human relationships; in *One of Ours,* Claude and Enid participate in an unnatural marriage that is essentially sexless, and their relationship fails because it grows out of ideals rather than realities. Finally, one critic employs the Ariel model to examine *The Song of the Lark*. The Ariel in American literature is the character who is incapable of establishing lasting human relationships because of self-centeredness and indifference. Ernest Earnest describes Thea Kronberg as the classic Ariel who is so selfish that she refuses to return home to see her dying mother because she would miss an important chance to sing. Yet, her indifference is perhaps even more reprehensible than her conceit. She is indifferent to those around her who are devoted to her; she uses people, perhaps unconsciously, to soothe her own troubled soul; and she manipulates the men in the novel without ever making a commitment.[86] Thea's life remains empty, because she cannot or does not enter into any meaningful relationships; her career, much like Alexandra's quest to tame the land, always gets in the way of meaningful personal encounters.

Nevertheless, the theme of failed human relationships occurs nowhere so strongly as it does in those short stories of Cather set on the prairie. In these stories, the lack of human relationships is coupled with the harsh frontier setting, and the result is isolation and loneliness. The pioneer valued independence and individualism, and the need to be able to rely only on oneself exaggerated the pioneer's isolation. The pioneers in Cather's short work are defeated and weary because of "an exacerbated sense of personal isolation and from the narrowing of all life to the individual's sensitivities. . . ."[87] Thus, the land on the frontier exaggerates and causes an acute sense of isolation for the pioneers who struggle to survive there; the lonely land itself heightens the pioneer's inability to enter into meaningful relationships.

Cather's early short stories, such as "Lou the Prophet," illustrate the grim isolation that occurs on the frontier and provides a glimpse at what life is like on the isolated frontier. These stories describe the "loneliness and hardship [that] can bring a person to the brink of insanity and sometimes even push him over. Lou is a young man driven to insanity by loneliness, deprivation, sorrow, and drought."[88] This quotation adequately describes the spirit of these early stories, which can best be illustrated by a short examination of "On the Divide."

In this story, Canute Canuteson is the "elemental man" who lives alone and who longs for human companionship. To alleviate his condition, he kidnaps a neighboring girl, forces the preacher to marry them, and then waits for the prairie loneliness to force her to accept him. These desperate actions exemplify the magnitude of the terrible loneliness that results from life on the isolated frontier and from the inability to maintain proper relationships in such an environment.[89]

The wide and relentless space on the lonely prairie keeps relationships from developing and tends to isolate the pioneers; yet, the characters who are isolated and marginal in the natural world can sometimes rise above the isolation that space imposes. Sometimes, in Cather's fiction, characters overcome their need to dominate the natural world, to secularize space, and turn their energies to relationships. In such instances, human beings overcome the alienating effects of space, if only for a short time, and experience the sacred significance of a life in harmony with the world and with the inhabitants of that world who surround them. Richard Giannone makes this point beautifully through his understanding of an event in Cather's short story, "Two Friends." In this story, two friends, Mr. Dillon and Mr. Trueman, witness with the narrator of the story an occultation of Venus. As the three of them watch, Venus and the moon seem to move together, become one, and then move apart again. This closing and then widening of space tells the symbolic story of the two friends and of relationships in Cather's fiction in general; the development of a meaningful relationship that closes the spaces between people is as rare, and often as short lived, as an occultation of Venus. "As with Venus and the moon, such crossings may happen only once in a lifetime."[90]

Nevertheless, such crossings do occur in Cather's fiction, and they form an alternative to the understanding of human existence in a Darwinian world that stresses physical laws and that ignores the value of spontaneous moments of human rapport. Some of Cather's characters overcome the need to give themselves to something "other" than meaningful human and natural relationships (usually the land). Some of her characters are able to learn from the sacred communities of the ancients or from the mystic occultation of Venus and enter into meaningful relationships with one another as well as with their natural environment. These triumphs occur with characters in such diverse works as *Alexander's Bridge, My Ántonia,* and *One Of Ours*.[91] Ántonia receives absolution in the end by establishing legitimate and fulfilling relationships with her husband and children, and Claude finally overcomes his disastrous home life through his ultimate friendship with David Gerhardt.

Cather's short stories help to illustrate the importance of relationships in her work. Lack of relationships tend to isolate persons while the establishment of relationships break through this isolation as in "The Diamond Mine." Cressida Garnet is one of the few Cather characters who recognizes the importance of relationships but who cannot enjoy a meaningful relationship because, like Alexandra, the drive for achievement and success hinders her. Cressida is strong willed, resolute, and successful like Alexandra and talented like Thea Kronberg, but she is unhappy because her success stands in the way of personal relationships. Finally she exclaims in frustration, "I have never cared about money, except to make people happy with it, and it has been the curse of my life. It has spoiled all my relations with people."[92]

Cressida appears in sharp contrast to a character like Marjorie (Margie) in "A Resurrection." Margie falls in love when she is very young to a river man, Martin Dempster. Nevertheless, Martin runs away and marries a French woman who gives him a child and who later drowns. In desperation, Martin returns to Margie, who rears his motherless child, and he finally admits his love for Margie who on Easter eve feels her love and desire for Martin resurrected. "Both age and isolation are defeated through the resurrection of love, ..." and through the establishment of relationships.[93] Finally, the story of Canute and his kidnapped mistress exemplifies the triumph that relationships render. In the end, Lena accepts the relationship with Canute and his isolation, as well as hers, ends.

A final short story, which emphasizes the importance of dramatic relationships with people as well as with one's environment, is "Neighbour Rosicky." This story recounts the gradual building of a relationship between Anton Rosicky and his daughter-in-law Polly. Polly is a town girl who experiences extreme isolation when she first moves to the prairie as Rudolph's (Rosicky's son) wife. Nevertheless, gradually, through acts of kindness, Rosicky endears himself to Polly. Ultimately, their relationship completely overcomes Polly's isolation when Rosicky has a fatal heart attack while working in Polly's field against his doctor's advice. For the first time since Polly's move to the frontier, she experiences wholeness and is able to call Rosicky "Father." The relationship they share overcomes Polly's isolation and makes her whole again.

Rosicky's life exemplifies what the lives of the ancient Indian tribes demonstrated—a harmonious existence that strikes a balance between harmony with the land and with people. Rosicky does not devote himself to making a fortune off the land because it would mean sacrificing his relationships with his family. A beautiful passage demonstrates the mutual love that Rosicky has for his family and the healthy relationship that he enjoys with the land. When a drought destroys his corn crop, he takes his family on a picnic without telling them the bad news. The tragedy crushes his neighbors, but Rosicky decides to enjoy his family and to revel in what they do have. He does not allow the struggle with the natural world to dictate the relationships that he has in his personal life, and because of this, his life is one of fulfillment and harmony that Dr. Ed's thoughts, at the end of the story, eulogize and recall.

> One soft, warm moonlight night in early summer he started for the farm. . . . Not until his road ran by the graveyard did he realize that Rosicky wasn't over there on the hill where the red lamplight shone, but here, in the moonlight. He stopped his car, shut off the engine, and sat there for a while. . . . Nothing could be more undeathlike than this place; nothing could be more right for a man who had helped to do the work of great cities and had always longed for the open country and had got to it at last. Rosicky's life seemed to him complete and beautiful.[94]

Finally, *O Pioneers!* provides perhaps the best example of healed relationships that overcome isolation, as the story ends with Alexandra's decision to marry her childhood friend, Carl Linstrum. She admits to Carl, "I needed you terribly. . . . You are all I have in the world. . . . I am tired, . . . I have been very lonely, Carl."[95] This decision inserts an element of harmony into the story after the disastrous affair of Emil and Marie. To the very end, Alexandra's life parallels the setting in which she exists: in her un-inhibited youth, the land is also wild; as she tames the land, she too experiences relative success, contentment, and inhibitions; after the ordeal with Emil and Marie, she grieves in a terrible storm; and as she and Carl insert an element of harmony to life late in their lives, the book ends with the harmonious setting of the sun and the rising of the evening star.

Nevertheless, the important point is that Alexandra's quest to conquer the land for Emil's behalf ends in tragedy, for she neglects relationships and cannot foresee the disaster as it approaches. The key to her fulfillment only comes at the end when she finally experiences harmony through the first meaningful relationship she experiences in her life—a relationship that materializes because of her own personal loss and tragedy.[96] Thus, Cather's fiction stresses that unnatural ways of relating lead to the inability of establishing meaningful human relationships, and as

Alexandra once again faces her land, it is with the assurance that fulfillment can exist only through a harmonious relationship with one's environment *and* with one's neighbors.

In *O Pioneers!*, an obsessive love of nature stands in the way of meaningful human relationships; therefore, successful interpersonal relations cannot happen for Cather unless one first understands the proper relationship one must maintain with the natural world. Thus, in a sense, nature makes human relationships possible. This relationship between nature and the social world is articulated in Wesley A. Kort's work on Joyce Carol Oates. A brief look at this relationship will help to clarify the vital link that exists in Cather's fiction between the natural and social worlds.

According to Kort, a "natural substructure" exists in the fiction of Joyce Carol Oates that makes healthy human relationships possible. Primary human relationships are a fundamental value in her fiction, and are possible only through a "wholesome, creative interdependence not only between individuals but also between people and their natural and historical environments."[97] Thus, the main factor for the "distortion of human relationships" is the "humanly created world" that makes life in harmony with the natural world virtually impossible. The human world offers "no support for the growth of human relationships or for the actualization of personal potential."[98] The problem is not that the human world is bad and the natural good; rather, the problem comes in the incompatibility of the two worlds to coexist—the social world and the natural are unnaturally separated.[99]

The same is true for Cather's fiction. Human relationships are primary in her work; however, her characters live in situations where obsession with either the natural world or the social world of human beings stands in the way of healthy relationships. The key is balance between the natural world and the social world and the realization that a proper approach to nature is necessary before one can enjoy meaningful relationships in the social world.

Thus, meaningful human relationships cannot exist except for the powerful role that the natural world exerts upon the human and social environment. As a result, the possibility of human potential emerges only through harmonious relationships with people and with the natural environment. The relationship between nature and society is such that isolation in the lonely world of nature and isolation in human relationships go hand in hand, while fulfilling relationships occur when one learns to approach nature respectfully without the urge to conquer and secularize it. For Cather, secularization destroys a sacred natural world and, thus, harmony; nevertheless, the negative effects of secularization can be balanced by harmony in the social sphere. In the relationship between the natural and human worlds, harmony begets harmony.

6. Summary

Willa Cather's fiction responds to the secularization of American space after the Darwinian revolution and to the threat it represents to the moral and spiritual moorings of Americans. Before Darwin, Americans considered themselves as the chosen of the universe; after Darwin, they were no longer the pinnacle of God's creation—they no longer could claim the benevolent garden as their home. As a result, Americans were forced to come to grips with new notions concerning the space that surrounded them, and Cather's fiction demonstrates how a person's world influences the direction of that person's life. Nevertheless, Cather's redefinition of American space goes beyond a mere acceptance of the Darwinian deterministic scenario. While the natural environment of Willa Cather's characters is antagonistic, it is not deterministic. She redefines the Darwinian world by rejecting the Darwinian laws of survival and by affirming the natural environment as an enabling context for proper human relationships. Yet, Willa Cather's fiction also counters a romantic view of natural space by painting a picture of nature as hostile, by reducing the centrality of characters in the created order, by stripping those characters of their sense of "home," and by picturing the land itself as "other." Nature is no longer simply a means to transcendent reality, but nature is also not simply a means toward the human goals of success and domination. Rather, nature is otherness itself, and it participates in satisfying the human longing for an existence legitimated by, or grounded in, something greater than human design or control.

The redefinition of natural space reveals stages of development in human attitudes toward natural space. First, harmony in a sacred setting occurs with the ancient people because they balance their reverence for the land and their love for one another. Second, the pioneers are noble, but their orientation secularizes nature because they attempt to subdue the land and because they neglect human companionship. Third, the farmers bring materialistic motives to the landscape and destroy reverence for what is natural. Finally, towns and cities emerge in the West and signal a disregard for the land. This secularization of natural space destroys the possibilities for a more fulfilling life in the West, and the result is disillusionment.

What are the positive contributions of nature to human life in Cather's fiction then? First, nature is unpredictable and large enough to strike awe in those able to acknowledge its power; second, nature is a stabilizing force because it grants humanity a sense of limitation; third, nature is capacious enough to provide the room for understanding and reconciliation between differing cultural groups (on the frontier, many cultural groups can live and work together in a common effort to survive the harshness of the natural world); fourth, nature is both beneficent and forbidding, and this ambiguous quality, along with awesome power, grants it a sense of otherness; and finally, nature makes constructive human relationships possible, for while the natural life alone is not sufficient, it is necessary for the emergence of personal fulfillment and wholesome relationships.

The principal belief advocated by Cather's fiction, then, is in the paradigm for human relationships that it implies: (1) harmonious communion with nature is the context for the peaceful existence with one's neighbor; (2) natural and cultural communion establishes harmony within the (at times) antagonistic natural settings; (3) such harmony reinvests human life with a significance that the constraints of a Darwinian universe prevents; (4) finally, the human element overcomes the secularizing impulses of American life—impulses that fail to recognize the potential for sacrality in a person's relation to natural environments and to personal relationships. In other words, in Cather's secular world, human relationships replace what one loses from the destruction of the sacred environment, namely a relationship with deity.

3

The Exorcism of the Supernatural

Natural and Social Alienation for Theodore Dreiser

There is little doubt that Theodore Dreiser's fiction constitutes an integral chapter in the American realistic and naturalistic literary movements. As a naturalistic philosopher, Dreiser may have been "a third-rate thinker," yet as a novelist, he can aptly be described as the "caretaker and janitor to the new century."[1] Dreiser's critics usually consider this "caretaker" role to be Dreiser's important contribution, because he helped to transform the direction of American literature.[2] This revolution in the literary world does insure his importance, but he is even more important because, like no other artist, he adeptly captured the imagination of Americans as social animals at the turn of the century. Dreiser had this impact because his fiction coincides with the end of a literary, philosophical, and religious ideology that dominated American writing throughout the nineteenth century.

Theodore Dreiser's fiction signals this end of an era through a redefinition of American space. In particular, Dreiser explores the consequences of the American social dream at the turn of the century and redefines social space. In the end he rejects the social dream of success and returns his thoughts to the natural world—to a natural world that is divested of the sacred categories imposed upon it by the romantics. Dreiser's work marks the end of the romantic worldview of sacred natural and social space; it redefines space in naturalistic terms; it reappropriates the American worldview in secular and social terms; it paints a picture of a social world that no longer provides access to otherness but one that is otherness itself.

In many ways, Dreiser did for social space in American fiction what Cather's work did for natural space. He tested the nineteenth-century optimistic assumptions concerning the social world, which were grounded in a sacred world conception, found them lacking, and discarded them for a secularized version of social space that avoids the conclusions of Darwinian determinism. Thus, whereas Cather's fiction relates the story of the seculariza- tion of the natural world, Dreiser's describes the secularization of social space, and, like Cather, Dreiser does not necessarily affirm this process but makes concessions to it in order to understand the modern world.

1. Introduction to the Study of Dreiser's Work: The Complexity of Theme

Since Dreiser's fiction marks the transition from one worldview to another, his work often oscillates between the two and presents a seemingly impossible web of confused thematic material. Never- theless, careful study reveals several fundamental implications that arise from his reassessment of the romantic view of the world. These basic themes in Dreiser's work help to explicate the move- ment in his novels as his work takes one from a past alien world (the sacred) to a more familiar world (the secular).

The first theme involves the exorcism of the supernatural from the natural world. The definition of sacred space revolves around the ability of that space to contain and to disclose "something of a wholly different order." In other words, sacred space allows for the "hierophany" of the transcendent or of the wholly "other."[3] This understanding of the world is a "way of being in the world" and gives humankind an existential point of reference around which to orient life.[4] This worldview undergirds the romantic concept of natural space, it dominates much of the writing of the nineteenth century, and it underlies the sacred understanding of the natural world that Dreiser's fiction redefines. This theme re- calls the same tendency found in Cather's work, yet in Dreiser's fiction, the focus contains much more devastating consequences for the social world.

In the redefinition that Dreiser's work represents, Dreiser does not focus upon transcendent reality but instead upon the imma- nent reality of "this 'real' world." Dreiser envisions a natural world that is "divested of its supernatural sanctions"[5]—a naturalistic world that completely destroys the notion that natural space is sa- cred. As a result, the natural world in Dreiser's fiction lacks a su- pernatural reality, and it no longer functions as the receptacle of or means to otherness. Instead, Dreiser creates an environment that is totally devoid of sacred significance—the natural world of Darwin.

The second theme revolves around the loss of a central belief that characterizes the disappearing sacred world. Since Dreiser's desacralized universe no longer contains the possibility of hierophantic experience, Dreiser's characters find themselves removed from the sacred garden and cast into a secular and impersonal environment. As a result, Dreiser's revision of the romantic worldview contains implications for the status of humanity and for the social world of nineteenth-century America. Dreiser's fiction concerns the problem of social innocence in the face of "the new national faith in an evolutionary universe."[6]

Evolutionary theory destroyed the idea of America as a "city upon a hill," and it made it impossible to believe that America and Americans were regarded as special in God's universe. As a result, the secularization of American natural space by the intrusion of the Darwinian world stripped nineteenth-century Americans of the supernatural essence that romanticism had granted them. At least one critic contrasts romantic literature and Dreiser's naturalism as opposites. Whereas romanticism "exalted man to the level of the Deity," naturalism "reduced man to the level of helplessness and ineffectualness [and] narrows to the vanishing point the gap separating man and the animals."[7] Thus, not only does Dreiser's fiction strip the natural world of sacred significance, it also invalidates the social world's claim to sacrality by reducing it to the level of the animal kingdom. This theme occurs in Cather's fiction as the peripheral existence of her frontier characters; however, in Dreiser's fiction, this vanishing point between the social and natural world, which makes humanity peripheral rather than central, is played out in the city instead of on the prairie.

The third basic theme in Dreiser's work develops from the second and involves the dislocation and alienation of Americans in a strange environment (marginality in Cather's fiction). The universe that Darwin introduces to popular America results in the alienation of humankind. The effect of this new conception of America removes Americans from the center of their paradisiacal land. Once men and women can no longer seek God in their natural world, they find themselves estranged and separated from the sacred world and its accompanying dream of opportunity, and they turn to the social environment in search of a new American vision. The result can be either despair or possibility; loneliness or peace. Like Cather, Dreiser writes about this human condition that afflicted the American people at the turn of the century, but for him, the social environment rather than the natural world enhances the American's feeling of isolation.

This characteristic of Dreiser's fiction leads to a fourth and crucial theme in his work—the secularization of American social space. Eighteenth-century Americans viewed themselves as the untarnished prophets of a new social vision, which in many ways became the urban parallel to the western dream of opportunity about which Cather writes; however, Dreiser destroys this notion by extending evolutionary theory beyond the biological realm and into the social realm. It should be no surprise that Dreiser read Spencer's theories with enthusiasm. This influence presents itself in Dreiser's fiction when the survival of the fittest applies to the way human beings relate in the social, communal world. This social natural selection occurs most clearly in Dreiser's impersonal and heartless urban environment, and, as a result, the city setting is integral to Dreiser's redefinition of the American dream and of American space.

As Dreiser's fiction turns to the social environment and to social concerns, his art takes on an autobiographical twist that becomes important for understanding the ambiguity that exists in his work. Dreiser's childhood environment seems to be an important force in the background of Dreiser's work. His family suffered an "ambiguous economic and social status," and Dreiser's "fear of poverty" put him in constant search "of the next higher social level."[8] This child who grew up in an ambiguous environment would mature into a man who wrote with an ambivalent attitude toward social setting.

Because Dreiser is uncertain about setting, it is only natural that his fiction tends to be dominated by environment or setting and by the limitations and opportunities that setting affords the individual and the social class.[9] Therefore, this study of Dreiser's fiction deals primarily with Dreiser's ambiguous use of setting as his novels seek a world where displaced Americans can once again feel at home. Such a world develops as setting (particularly the city environment) emerges as a religiously significant category that both 1) makes human growth and potential a reality and that 2) threatens to relegate humanity to ambiguity. Because of this dual nature of setting, the environment (especially the social world) replaces the transcendent as that which is "other" than humanity and as that which controls the destinies of individuals.

This conception of setting as "other" presents itself most clearly in Dreiser's ambiguous conception of the city, and this idea makes up a fifth basic theme of Dreiser's work—the idea of the environment as that which satisfies humanity's need for otherness. In Dreiser's fiction, the city is the new setting where the American dream either fails or succeeds. This new American dream in the urban environment emerges as the ability to realize social and financial success shifts from the rural landscape to the urban setting. Such a shift identifies the city as the place of opportunity, yet it also shows the city as the environment that can crush one with complete anonymity. Thus, the city, for Dreiser, parallels Cather's frontier in that it creates an acute crisis for Americans—an identity crisis that, for Dreiser, begins in the city for urban Americans desperately seeking a new home in the grasp of an industrialized nation.

The changing conception of the American dream, its transition from rural heartland to urban streets, the redefinition of social space, the dehumanization of human relationships, and the negative impact upon the identity of Americans constitute prominent themes in Dreiser's fiction. These forces result in the destruction of the new American vision that revolved around social success and space; yet, Dreiser does not reject the American dream itself. Rather, he reappropriates it in terms of a desacralized natural world. His enlightened view of the natural world provides meaning that he could find neither in the sacred natural world of the romantics nor in the competitive social world of the industrialized city. Thus, Dreiser's view of the natural world, which in turn sheds light upon social reality, constitutes a sixth theme that is crucial to his fiction.

This sixth major theme allows the natural world, with its brutish emphasis on Darwinian philosophy, to inform and critique social reality. With his movement to and emphasis upon social criticism, it is easy to see why Dreiser's work is so unsettling and disturbing. He is concerned not with telling a soothing story but with telling the truth. Dreiser wants "to tell life as it is . . . —the facts as they exist, the game as it is played."[10] This naturalistic insistence upon the truth threatens because it focuses upon "the tragedy of man's life" without massaging his fragile ego.[11] Thus, in Dreiser's fiction, the old standards that dominate the romantic vision surrender to the disturbing advent of a Darwinian world and to Dreiser's own need to faithfully render life as he saw it (this is a characteristic that Dreiser shared with Cather and the other realists). Dreiser described his own agenda in the following way:

Ladies and gentlemen, this has been my vision of life. This is what living in my time has seemed to be like. . . . You may not like my vision, ladies and gentlemen, but it is the only one I have seen and felt, and, therefore, it is the only one I can give you.[12]

Thus, although Dreiser seems "certain of nothing," he continues his ambiguous "seeking without a finding"[13] as he reports upon American society in search of a social truth gleaned from

natural laws. It is at this point that so many critics err in reading
and interpreting Dreiser. It is easy to ascribe the evolutionary philosophy of survival of the fittest to Dreiser. It is tempting to say
that Dreiser was ruthless and that he advocated the survival of the
fittest and the richest in society, because the fit usually prosper
in his novels and because this would constitute a natural progres-
sion from the law of nature to the law of society. But it is quite
clear that this Spencerian philosophy is not one that Dreiser advocates; rather, he is simply describing the laws that his world seems
to acknowledge and embrace. Thus, "the gospel according to
Theodore Dreiser" is not the "complete amoralism" of a naturalistic philosophy as Randall Stewart and others would like to
suggest.[11]

Rather, the Cowperwood philosophy that dominates his trilogy—
the "I satisfy myself" attitude to life—is not the philosophy
of Dreiser. The Cowperwood philosophy "by no means represents Dreiser's views, and his contemporary critics went far astray
in ascribing to him a philosophy paralleling his hero's."[15] Thus,
Dreiser is not the ruthless Spencerian that he is often considered
to be but a compassionate and troubled man who weeps over life's
problems. This is the Theodore Dreiser who is troubled by the
injustice of the world and who tries to capture that injustice in
his art; this is the Dreiser who writes about a world where the supernatural is no longer present and that operates by the laws of
natural selection and survival of the fittest; this is the man whose
fiction participates in a transition in the attitude toward American
space from sacred to secular conceptions.

Why is Dreiser unable to think of the world in sacred terms?
Why does Dreiser's description of America picture a world devoid
of the transcendent and ruled by the impersonal forces of the natural realm? Obviously Dreiser is greatly affected by the evolutionary theory of Darwin and Spencer, yet there is a more intimate
explanation for Dreiser's inability to think of the world in sacred
terms. This explanation is a product of the passionate Dreiser
who cannot deal with the possibility of God in the world because
of the gross injustice that he senses around him.

Dreiser's inability to conceive of a benevolent God in a cruel
world suggests a seventh major theme that is the beginning point
for Dreiser's fiction—a theme that states the classical problem of
theodicy. Dreiser's work does not accept the notion that God is
the creator of "the best of all possible worlds,"[16] according to Alfred Kazin. Kazin implies that the classical formulation of the
problem of evil plagues Theodore Dreiser. With all the evil and

injustice that he sees in his America, Dreiser cannot believe that a benevolent and a just God is present and active in the world of men and women. Instead, he describes a world absented by God and ruled by the ruthless laws of evolution.

Dreiser's struggle with theodicy occurs throughout his work and is the basis for his rejection of the romantic sacramental view of the universe. The problem seems to stem from his early religious exposure to traditional Roman Catholicism. Dreiser confesses that Roman Catholic dogma does not satisfactorily explain life for him, and he reconciles this problem by rejecting the traditional view of God. The Catholic God cannot exist in the world for Dreiser,[17] and he extends his own struggle with the problem of evil from his autobiography to his fiction. In *An American Tragedy*, Clyde Griffiths struggles with the problem of evil early. Clyde knows that his family is deprived—"always 'hard up,' never very well clothed, and deprived of many comforts and pleasures which seemed common enough to others." Clyde believes that conditions should not be so harsh if God is present and is as merciful as his pious parents proclaim; he knows that there is "something wrong somewhere." Even Clyde's mother expresses this same doubt of God's benevolent providence when she is faced with Esta's disappearance. In her moment of need "her God, her Christ" abandoned her when "obvious evil was being done."[18] Clyde's struggle represents just one example from many of Dreiser's treatment of theodicy. From his early work to *The Bulwark* and *The Stoic*, Theodore Dreiser struggles with the ancient problem of evil, and the result of this struggle is Dreiser's description of a world where God neither resides nor works.

It is crucial to note here the similarity of Cather's and Dreiser's literary quests for truth. Cather's fiction begins with a concern for and results in the secularization of natural space, yet this process is informed by the social world and human relationships. In contrast, Dreiser's fiction is dominated by the secularization of social space, yet it is tempered by his view of the natural world. Even though each author begins with different concerns and with different subjects, they both end up affirming an wholistic view of the world based on social and natural harmony.

2. Unity in Dreiser's Bipolar Ambiguity

These themes suggest divergent tendencies in Dreiser's fiction. On the one hand, Dreiser's work is a literary expression of America's encounter with Darwin's scientific universe; and on the other hand, Dreiser's fiction stands as a transition point in American literature as the romantic tradition of the nineteenth century finally capitulates to literary naturalism. As a result, the themes that Dreiser develops do not create any type of systematic thought or philosophy. Thus, just as Cather paints an ambiguous attitude toward the frontier, so is Dreiser's fiction ambiguous and sometimes seemingly contradictory. He often seems to waver between deterministic and free-will theories concerning human nature. Nevertheless, there is an underlying and uniform pattern to Dreiser's bifurcated vision that helps to explicate the ambiguity that has frustrated critics for almost a century. This critical confusion results in the assumptions that Dreiser's literature and philosophy are the same and that his thought is dualistic in nature. Neither of these assumptions is necessarily true.[19]

Nevertheless, Dreiser's work is not hopelessly confused in a web of dualistic themes. An insightful article by Charles Child Walcutt, "Theodore Dreiser and the Divided Stream," helps to explicate Dreiser's ambiguous dualism. Walcutt traces Dreiser's ambiguity to the disintegration of Emersonian Transcendentalism. What for Emerson is a monistic philosophical system where "Nature reveals and embodies Spirit" breaks down with the decline of transcendentalism.[20] Dreiser inherits this divided monism that still contains Emerson's two elements of spirit and nature but that also places these elements in opposition to one another. Thus, sometimes Dreiser emphasizes the natural component and writes from a pessimistic, naturalistic vantage point; yet, at other times the spiritual component possesses Dreiser and he writes with a realistic strain of hope.[21]

Walcutt's construction is the most helpful for understanding Dreiser's ambiguity. The remainder of this chapter is the elaboration of my attempt to understand the literature of Theodore Dreiser not as dualistic but as unified—as a complex description of the American dream in the social environment. The argument that follows develops in two stages that describe two poles in Dreiser's art, which cooperate to form a unified understanding of America. The first pole in Dreiser's fiction is a description of a world dominated by Darwinian materialism and Spencerian philosophy. This deterministic and mechanistic pole develops in his fiction in the form of individualism and the survival of the fittest and occurs in the setting of the social environment. Some of the works that are dominated by this pole are *Sister Carrie, The Financier,* and *The Titan.* The second pole of Dreiser's thought is pietistic naturalism.

This philosophical stance allows one to approach the natural world and the social environment with piety without denying the naturalistic forces at work in the universe. *The Bulwark* and *The Stoic* are two works that are dominated by Dreiser's pietistic naturalism.[22]

These two phases or poles of Dreiser's thought are not simply opposites, because they both participate in Dreiser's exorcism of the supernatural from the world of humankind and in the development of his view of social space in secular terms. Rather, they appear as two manifestations (within the narrative component) of the same type of movement away from a sacred conception of the universe. For example, Darwinian materialism resembles a Calvinistic determinism without God, and pietistic naturalism parallels a religious pietism without the supernatural. Furthermore, one should not consider these two poles of Dreiser's fiction in simply developmental or chronological terms but as having a dialogical component as well. Both poles are present throughout Dreiser's fiction, which oscillates from one pole to the other, as the two poles inform and challenge one another. Sometimes the Darwinian pole dominates to describe the social world as Dreiser sees it—a world filled with hopelessness and pessimism. At other times the pietistic pole dominates to describe the natural world and the social environment as it should be approached—a world tempered by an idealistic optimism.

Nevertheless, the two poles are present throughout; they both emerge from Dreiser's consuming desire to solve the problem of theodicy; they both cooperate in the reappropriation of the romantic, sacramental worldview. As a result, the two poles combine to create a secular universe where God does not live and, thus, where the problem of evil no longer exists. Dreiser's fictional world resolves these dilemmas as it comes to grips with biological and social determinism through a natural explanation, and as a result of this, Dreiser is often viewed as a champion of Darwinian and Spencerian theory.

However, those critics, who insist upon viewing Dreiser as "a purely mechanical naturalist,"[23] fail to recognize that although naturalistic and deterministic philosophies play an important role in Dreiser's fiction, his naturalism is qualified by an interest in spiritual, moral, and humanitarian concerns. This limited naturalism allows Dreiser to break with tradition and to impart a particular American quality to his work[24]—an American quality that arises from Dreiser's thought concerning the American dream of opportunity and that emanates from the sacred construction of

social reality. Thus, as Cather redefined the sacred world construction and the dream of opportunity surrounding the natural
world, Dreiser qualifies the sacred dream in connection with social space by tempering his naturalism with moral standards.
These humanistic and moral concerns arise in a later discussion
of Dreiser's pietistic naturalism; however, first Dreiser's struggle
with the Darwinian natural world and the Spencerian social world
shall be examined as a precursor to his later reappropriation of
more traditional attitudes toward American natural and social
space.

3. Darwinian and Spencerian Naturalism in Dreiser's Fiction

The first pole of Dreiser's fiction evolves naturally from the
Darwinian expulsion of God from the universe, and it develops
in his fiction as a movement from biological to social determinism.
As mentioned in chapter 1, the advent of Darwinism and its reception on a popular level resulted in the secularization of both
the natural and social worlds for Americans. Dreiserian determinism has a similar effect in his fiction that presupposes a world
where human beings are alienated and alone—a world where
men and women live by animal desire—a world where persons
are tossed about by turns of fate and chance—the world that is
described at the beginning of chapter 8 in *Sister Carrie*. In this environment, human beings lose their identity because they do not
have complete control of their lives. Rather, the awesome power
of natural forces over human will overshadows the little freedom
that they do possess.

> Among the forces which sweep and play throughout the universe, un-
> tutored man is but a wisp in the wind . . . moved by every breath of
> passion, acting now by his will and now by his instincts. . . . We have
> the consolation of knowing that evolution is ever in action. . . .[25]

Yet, what consolation is it to know that the process of evolution
controls the destiny of humankind? Darwin shows that the evolutionary process operates by the principle of the survival of the
fittest. Thus, does Dreiser really think it consoling to know that
the weak will be crushed in order to strengthen the strong?
This is the dilemma that the first phase of Dreiser's thought
presupposes—the dilemma that can be solved only by Dreiser's
superman.

Dreiser's adaption of Darwinism in the form of the superman focuses upon the concept of the survival of the fittest and is best illustrated by his famous lobster and squid passage. In *The Financier,* young Frank Cowperwood observes a lobster and a squid that are in the same tank at a fish market. Frank watches daily as the lobster pursues and finally kills the squid. The incident causes Frank to ask the question, "'How is life organized?'" His answer is,

> That's the way it has to be, I guess. . . . That squid wasn't quick enough. . . . The squid couldn't kill the lobster—he had no weapon. The lobster could kill the squid—he was heavily armed. There was nothing for the squid to feed on; the lobster had the squid as prey. What was the result to be? What else could it be? He didn't have a chance. . . .[26]

This event is profoundly disturbing for Frank because it causes him to question the purpose of life. Frank finds meaning in the Darwinian principle that only the strong will survive, and he eventually survives and succeeds through strength at the expense of the weak. Thus is born the superman, Cowperwood.

Dreiser's concept of the superman emerges to dominate his Cowperwood trilogy. The superman alone (Cowperwood) is strong and ruthless enough to succeed in a Darwinian world. In contrast is a character like Clyde Griffiths, who is weak and helpless and who dies prematurely because he is incapable of dealing with the cruelties of life. Thus, Cowperwood, as "a man who recognizes no restraints or limits and . . . who illustrates the limitations of all men," is the epitome of Dreiser's conception of the strong who survive in a secular universe.[27] This is the Cowperwood of *The Titan,* who comes "by degrees to take on the outlines of a superman, a half-god or demi-Gorgon."[28]

The same forces that allow a Cowperwood to succeed also operate to enslave the mass of human beings to a blind, mechanistic fate. Thus, Dreiser is interested in the natural characteristics that make a person either strong or weak and that necessarily reap consequences in the social world as well. As a result of this dual interest, Dreiser's determinism develops in two directions. The first is biological determinism that operates through Dreiser's chemic principle, and the second is social determinism that comes from Dreiser's reading of Herbert Spencer.[29]

Both branches of Dreiser's determinism have different emphases; however, they both have a common grounding. They both presuppose that humanity is controlled by some larger force, and as a result, men and women are insignificant parts of the world where they live. Robert Elias quotes Arthur Henry from *An Island Cabin* as Henry attempts to describe Dreiser's conception of an individual's place in the universe. The universe is not a great man like

> a Bismarck, a Gladstone, a Morgan or a Rockefeller. . . . It is just an average, rather phlegmatic sort of fellow, preserving a formal, well-balanced poise in mediocrity, . . . and man [is] but a minor subdivision in its make-up.[30]

This idea of the radical insignificance of humankind develops from Dreiser's ideas of biological and social determinism and is characteristic of secularizing forces in the nineteenth century. Whereas in Cather's fiction, otherness, which leads to the insignificance of humanity, appears as the landscape, in Dreiser's work, it is either biological chemisms or the social structure that becomes ultimate.

Dreiser's characters are helpless on an individual level because they are controlled by natural forces through biological determinism. Robert Elias demonstrates the sovereignty of nature in his classic work *Theodore Dreiser: Apostle of Nature*. Elias says that in Dreiser's short fiction, the motto "nature must prevail . . ." appears as the dominant thesis. His stories "show that individuals . . . [are] limited by circumstances or feelings . . ." that are the responsibility of "an inscrutable and indifferent nature." Elias quotes Dreiser from "The Myth of Individuality" in order to substantiate his statement.

> "By reason of creation, man is not only made but controlled by nature or creation, his thought is its thought; his reactions its reactions. . . . Apart from it . . . he has no existence. . . ."[31]

This biological determinism appears in Dreiser's fiction in the form of chemisms. Dreiser adapts the Loebian concept of chemical mechanism to describe how individuals are simply the slaves of the natural universe.[32] Clyde Griffiths is the ultimate victim to chemic forces in *An American Tragedy*[33] as he is helpless before his sexual and societal needs. These driving forces are in turn simply a result of certain chemical combinations that constitute Clyde's desires.

Examples of chemic determinism appear frequently in Dreiser's fiction; however, two examples serve to illustrate this natural determinism. The first example comes from Dreiser's play, *The Hand of the Potter*, and is an elaboration of a statement that Dreiser makes in his autobiography, *Newspaper Days*. In his autobiography, Dreiser comments that human beings are made a certain way for which they are not responsible, and he develops this thesis in his play through the character of Isodore. Isodore is the pathetic victim of some chemical imbalance that causes an abnormal sex drive. Isodore is attracted to little girls, and before the play ends he molests and kills a young girl and commits suicide to escape guilt. However, Dreiser does not hold Isodore responsible for his crime, because Isodore is the victim of the capricious character of nature that makes him perverted. Isodore exclaims, "I didn't make myself, did I?," and the reader forgives him because he is as much a victim of nature as he is a criminal.[34]

A second example from *Sister Carrie* demonstrates that nature is sovereign and whimsical—it can smile on some and can just as quickly destroy their good fortune. Carrie's success is predicated upon her natural beauty. Because of a random quirk in the natural process, Carrie is endowed with a physical appearance that opens the gate for her into the "walled city." Bob Ames, a potential suitor, points out to Carrie that her face is her success; she has "paid nothing to get it." However, the natural process that grants Carrie an initial advantage also strips her of that advantage through the aging process. Bob Ames assures Carrie that she will age and lose her seductive beauty; "nature takes care of that."[35] The same process happens to Aileen in *The Titan*. Her beauty fades as she grows older, heavier, and less attractive to Cowperwood. In the end, nature destroys the random advantage that it bestows in the first place, and it demonstrates its sovereignty over the destinies of human beings. Carrie's beauty is reminiscent of Marian Forrester in Cather's *A Lost Lady*. In both cases, the Darwinian laws, which allow individuals to struggle with and triumph over the forces of nature, fail to fully explain the individual's true dependency upon nature.

Natural forces that control men and women appear in many different forms in Dreiser's novels; nevertheless, the main force in nature is closely tied to chemic forces and comes in the guise of unfulfilled desire. Although desire in the human animal manifests itself in forms ranging from animal lusts to the need for social acceptance and prominence, Dreiser's philosophy usually begins on the basic level of sexual desire and instinctual lust. Dreiser even admits that his own burden in life is his unfulfilled and frustrated sex drive. With the realization that his sexual goal will probably not be obtained without marriage, he makes the following comment in his autobiography:

> I felt like one condemned to carry a cross. . . . I suffered untold tortures from my desires and my dreams. And they were destined never to be fulfilled. . . . Glorious fruit that hangs upon the vine too long, and then decays.[36]

Dreiser does not look to nature for a divine encounter as did the romanticists before this; rather, he seeks in nature relief from and satisfaction of his own narcissistic "pagan passion."[37]

Dreiser develops his philosophy of sex in the Cowperwood trilogy. Throughout the trilogy, Cowperwood collects and discards lovers in response to his own selfish sexual appetite. Cowperwood's sexual exploits approach a metaphysical state and an aesthetic ideal at times; however, sex usually appears as a "pagan passion" and is described in terms of animal desire. The same Darwinian forces that compel human beings to fight for survival also drive them to the need to satisfy themselves sexually and in every other way.

> Men killed to live—all of them—and wallowed in lust in order to reproduce themselves. In fact, wars, vanities, pretenses, cruelties, greeds, lusts, murder, spelled their true history, with only the weak running to a mythical saviour or god for aid. And the strong using this belief in a god to further the conquest of the weak.[38]

Thus, the strong have no need for the supernatural in a Darwinian world except to satisfy their own needs and natural desires, and the weak can only look to nature in despair as the captor and master of their will. In either case, unfulfilled natural urges and desires lead to social maladjustment and problems.

Dreiser's fictional environment reveals this attitude toward sex and desire as a narcissistic philosophy—a philosophy that holds desire and nature as the chief instigators in humanity's quest to seek self gratification. Again, Cowperwood is the main example of a life controlled by desire for immediate gratification. His philosophy is summarized in his motto for living; "I satisfy myself" is the rule that governs Cowperwood's life, and he follows it faithfully regardless of the consequences to other people.[39] As a result, Cowperwood is able to discard Aileen and a myriad of other lovers when a new star shines on the horizon.

This approach to life is elaborated upon in *An American Tragedy* but with different results. Clyde Griffiths is not a superman like Frank Cowperwood; however, Clyde is consumed by the same attitude toward life—an attitude that states "I satisfy myself" sexually, socially, and materialistically. This Darwinian or Spencerian urge leads to the confused and cowardly Clyde who plots Roberta's death and who watches her die. And in the end, it is this narcissistic urge that causes Clyde to cry in his jail cell. He cries not in remorse but from the frustration of failure for his own plans and desires.

Nevertheless, even though this philosophy of life is prominent in Dreiser's fiction, it is incorrect to suggest that Dreiser advocates such an attitude. Dreiser is not moralizing but is attempting to report the truth as he sees it, and this true state of humankind is the state of Darwinian enslavement. In fact, Dreiser may mourn over this fact instead of thinking it admirable, because it only frustrates and leads to tragedy. Cowperwood and Lester Kane die frustrated men; Clyde dies in the electric chair; and in the revised ending of *Sister Carrie*, Dreiser comments upon the inevitable end that must follow when one lives life in search of self-satisfaction.

> Know, then, that for you is neither surfeit nor content. In your rocking chair, by your window dreaming, shall you long, alone. In your rocking chair, by your window, shall you dream such happiness as you may never feel.[40]

This deterministic tendency in Dreiser's fiction is not limited to Darwinian determinism that affects human beings on the individual and biological level. Dreiser also writes about humanity on a collective and social level. In fact, even when Dreiser's fiction deals with individual determinism in the form of chemisms, in actuality, he writes about humanity as a social phenomenon, because chemisms ultimately determine how human beings relate socially to one another. Thus, it is not surprising when Dreiser attempts "to identify social forces, to grasp them, and to correlate them with human destiny" as he concentrates on "social history, the social processes of evil."[41]

However, as with his treatment of the natural world, Dreiser does not advocate a particular social reality. Rather, he attempts to describe and report the true social reality of America. His social criticism is a subtle one related through his "patient and meticulous skill at analysis," and it is fundamental to his understanding of America and the American dream in the latter part of the nineteenth century. Dreiser, like Cather, is never quite comfortable with the effects of secularization, yet he describes those effects in order to deal with them more realistically. His fiction reveals a criticism based upon the Darwinian and Spencerian "conviction that physical, economic and social environment, and not strength of character, nor divine intervention determines the fate of man."[42] Thus, Dreiser's understanding of social space, like his picture of the natural realm and like Cather's reluctant description of her own world, is one devoid of supernatural reality. Dreiser's fictional social world mirrors the obsolescence of the romantic sacred worldview, and it helps to create a new understanding of the social world where reality is not measured by transcendent intrusion. In other words, Dreiser's world emerges from secular, social space that operates according to the same Darwinian laws that govern the natural world and that left nineteenth-century Americans in a confused and desperate dilemma.

It is appropriate to follow an examination of Dreiser's understanding of the natural realm with an analysis of his construction of the social world, because in his own fiction the natural, physical environment tends to determine and mirror the social environment and social relationships. Thus, the struggle that individuals face with natural, biological desires and lusts translates into the social, communal world through frustrated and confused interpersonal relationships. The competitive, natural world of Darwin imposes itself upon the social realm, and it destroys the possibility of meaning in social relationships. The physical world and the chemic principle are in constant conflict with social space, and the result is that environment and setting play a deterministic role in Dreiser's fiction. At this point, the fiction of Dreiser shows an intimate resonance with Spencerian determinism, and he often flaunts his reading of Spencer's philosophy in his autobiography. Therefore, the survival of the fittest in the social world is a major theme for Dreiser and appears when social forces in the environment enslave and victimize individuals.

An intense social dilemma emerges from Dreiser's view of secular society, and it destroys the founding fathers' social vision of America. For Dreiser, traditional American society does not allow for any meaningful realization of the American success dream because it creates a "no win" situation. The American dream places great emphasis upon individual achievement, yet traditional mores continually suppress the ability of the individual to act upon his or her personal desires and dreams. Thus, if one realizes social success and the "ideals of society," that person is ostracized from society, because success requires ruthless self-interest (sur-

vival of the fittest) and acts that are condemned by society. However, if one does not realize success, then that person does not
realize the ideals of society and is a failure. The result is that
"Dreiser's novels take place in a society that is itself constantly
passing judgment on its members. It is a society in conflict with
itself over the values it actually lives by and those it thinks it lives
by." Furthermore, this dilemma is the result of the substitution
of the "demands of society" for the will of God.[43] Thus, Dreiser
describes a society that makes itself supreme and ultimate—a society that is otherness itself. Yet, this "other" reality is schizophrenic
in its demands, and it frustrates individuals who are controlled
by its whimsical sovereignty.

Because social forms enslave and control the lives of individuals
in Dreiser's fiction, and because they are ambiguous and contradictory, social forces are not meaningful—they do not allow personal expression. Society dictates the actions of its members
rather than allowing divergence from traditional social mores and
restrictions. Such an expression of individuality results in disaster.
In *Jennie Gerhardt,* the conventional standards of society both dictate Jennie's life and work to destroy her. Because of her poverty
and social standing, Jennie is forced to give herself sexually to
Senator Brander and to Lester Kane. Yet, it is also social convention that prevents Jennie from marrying either Brander or Lester.
Although Lester admits that Jennie is "the only woman . . . [he]
ever did love truly," social expectations concerning class and success drive Lester to marry Mrs. Gerald so that "he would have the
satisfaction of knowing that this Western social and financial
world . . . [would hold] no more significant figure than himself."[44]
Thus, Lester chooses social affluence over love and dies un-
happily. Furthermore, he leaves Jennie in a state of social
ostracism—a state that she suffers because of her poverty and her
extra-marital sexual activity. Social convention serves to favor
those who are worthy but repress those who do not meet socially
acceptable standards. Darwinian standards of survival of the fittest are operative even beyond the biological realm in the world
of interpersonal relationships, and they appear in the form of social desires that stand in the way of meaningful personal relationships.

These constraining forces of society, the dominance of fate and
circumstances, and the seductive lure of power represent what
Kazin calls "the underside of American life" in Dresier's fiction.
This dark side of the American success dream requires a whole
new ethical and moral system, because "the middle-class morality

of the nineteenth century" is grossly inadequate to confront the problems of a changing America.[45] The inadequacy of traditional social and religious standards lies at the bottom of *An American Tragedy*. Even though Clyde is a victim to his own narcissistic desires, he is also an innocent victim to an outdated and dominating moral system.

The beginning of the novel carefully sketches Clyde's early home environment as Dreiser presents the reader with a pathetic family dominated by a narrow and restrictive religious fanaticism. Clyde's childhood is grossly inadequate to prepare him for life, and as a result, Clyde does not possess the necessary skills to function in the societal world of grand hotels and of prestigious Lycurgus. Dreiser's fiction criticizes the church as the harbinger of society's traditional creeds, and he condemns the blind "acceptance of [society's] dogmas, its superstitions, its ideals." Thus, Clyde's crime is not "for rebelling against the established social order" but "for *not* rebelling against it."[46]

There is yet a second way that society victimizes Clyde and renders him helpless to forces beyond his control. "American society, as Dreiser saw it, furnished Clyde with no standard save that of wealth, ease and social position."[47] The American dream as applied to social space and standing is a dream of status and prestige. Thus, Clyde is victim to the desires that society itself places upon him; he cannot help himself. He does not marry Roberta because that would mean losing his chance at a relationship with Sondra and, thus, with social status. Roberta's death and Clyde's tragedy, then, happen for two reasons. First, the traditional moral code of society is not sufficient to prepare Clyde for the complexity of societal relationships; second, society itself is to blame for victimizing its members with the irresoluble dilemma that it creates for its members. In the end, Clyde is a helpless victim to the forces of the social world that are beyond his control.

This is the state of social reality in the latter nineteenth century as it appears in Dreiser's fiction. His social criticism evolves from his understanding of the success oriented American dream and from his belief that this dream "had degenerated into *Tragic America*."[48] Much of his social criticism emerges from his copious reading of Herbert Spencer and his attempt to make sense of his environment in the post-Darwinian world where he lived. Thus, Dreiser's picture of social space appears, not surprisingly, in the form of Spencerian determinism. Dreiser uses Spencer as an "explanation of experience" to describe the forces that take place in societal relationships,[49] yet Dreiser is selective in his acceptance of

Spencerian doctrine. He accepts the concept of survival of the fittest as operative, but he cannot believe that progress is guaranteed or predictable. He cites the advent of industrialism as the force that negates Spencer's doctrine of progress.[50] Furthermore, Dreiser does not apply his Spencerian leanings to the legitimation of capitalism that Spencer's doctrines usually support. Thus, this assessment of Dreiser's debt to Spencerian philosophy comes in two stages. First, Dreiser uses the concept of survival of the fittest positively to explain what he envisions as a ruthless society; second, negatively, Dreiser does not follow the logical outcome of Spencerian doctrine to an endorsement of unbridled capitalism.

Dreiser's first point, the ruthless, Spencerian social world, arises from the settings for his novels. These settings are "depersonalized and predatory" environments and are made up of exploiters and the exploited—the Cowperwoods and the Clyde Griffiths.[51] For Dreiser, the social setting operates by Darwinian rules, and he describes it with Darwinian language.

> In distant ages . . . a minute cellular organism [evolved] . . . and had finally learned to organize itself into man. Man, on his part, composed as he was of self-organizing cells, was pushing himself forward into comfort and different aspects of existence by means of union and organization with other men.[52]

The same forces of evolution, which work in the natural world to ensure that the strong flourish, extend into the social organization of human beings and explain social reality, relationships, and organization.

Dreiser provides three poignant images that illustrate this understanding of social organization in his essay, "A Lesson from the Aquarium." Dreiser describes the antics of minnows, hermit crabs, and shark-suckers to underscore the way that humans act toward one another. In the minnow colony, some of the minnows act as guards to keep the others from eating the eggs, yet when the eggs hatch, the guards go off duty and they become predators for the next group of eggs. "Their roles as guardians of public morality are for the time discontinued." Likewise, in the human world there are those who only guard their own self-interest and who desire to seize that which is not theirs. A second lesson from the aquarium revolves around the hermit crab, which is born unprotected and which only gets a home when he takes a shell from a weaker sea creature. And as the crab grows, "it is necessary for him to make another sortie; and you may frequently see in this tank the operation of the law of the survival of the fittest, that makes our world so grim." The third lesson comes from the shark-sucker, which is a weak parasite that attaches itself to a shark and feeds on the food that falls from the shark's mouth. If this parasite is separated from the shark it will lie on the bottom of the tank and starve to death before it will actively seek food. Dreiser suggests that there are people in society who are just as weak and lazy and content to live off the fortunes of others. Thus, in this essay, Dreiser paints the condition of humankind in terms of the animal kingdom and the process of evolution.

> Do not these examples furnish excellent illustration of our own physical and social condition? What set of capitalists, or captains of industry, think you, controlling a fine privilege or franchise, which they wish to hatch into a large fortune would not envy the stout minnows their skill in driving enemies away? What sharper prowling about and viewing another's comfortable home, or his excellent business, or the beauty of his wife, if the desire seized him, would not seize upon one or all of these, and by a process of mental gymnastics, or physical force, not unlike that of the hermit crab, endeavor to secure for himself the desirable shell? What weakling, seeing the world was against him, and that he was not fitted to cope with it, would not attach himself, sucker-wise, to any magnate, trust, political or social (we will not call them sharks), and content himself with what fell from his table? ... Bless us, how closely these lesser creatures do imitate us in action—or how curiously we copy them![53]

For Dreiser, social human acts like the animals, and his picture of social organization contrasts sharply with that of the romantic poets who view humans as drawing close to supernatural reality.

This last quotation suggests the second characteristic of Dreiser's adapted Spencerian philosophy. Dreiser's conception of social space does not condone capitalism, because he sees it as the system that allows economic and social injustice and that creates the type of social dilemma that leads to Clyde Griffith's "American" tragedy. For Dreiser, capitalism itself is not bad, and it was the best system for a new nation struggling with democracy. However, Dreiser's fictional, social environment suggests that by the end of the nineteenth century, capitalism was insufficient to meet the demands of an industrializing nation. Capitalism in the 1890s, which allows the financiers to prosper while the mass of people suffer injustice and poverty, is the system that Dreiser writes about—the system that leads to Clyde's frustration, Hurstwood's decline, and Cowperwood's rise and fall.[54]

Dreiser's picture of social space is one of a deterministic environment—an environment that is Spencerian and Darwinian in intent and cruelly outdated for changing America. And for most of his fiction, this environment takes place in the city setting. The dynamics of the city play an important role in the social dynamics of Dreiser's work as he explores the meaning of urban space. The meaning of the city, like Dreiser's caricature of society in general and of the natural world, applies to human life on two levels. On the one hand, the city is organized to test the limits of the individual. In this sense, human life is similar to animal life, and survival of the fittest reigns in the city streets to test the strength of the individual. However, animal life also possesses a communal side. Thus, on the other hand, the city is organized spatially in order to promote collective life, yet it makes social life almost impossible by relegating most persons to anonymity. This tension creates a fruitful paradox for Dreiser's work where the city, like nature for Cather, fosters ambiguity and uncertainty for its inhabitants.

This ambiguity in Dreiser's novels revolves around an exchange of social space in America. Although the family farm and the yeoman farmer are central to the fiction of his contemporary, Willa Cather, they are relics of the past for Dreiser; and the city ushers in a new social environment, new social forms, and new social expectations with new promises. The horizon of the American city is the setting of Dreiser's work, because he recognizes that the small community is outdated for an industrial nation. However, he does not ignore the fact that the small community, the family farm, and the social forms prior to the rise of urban centers provide stability and security that the seething and growing city can never imitate. Dreiser's work articulates a revolutionary change in American life. For example, *Sister Carrie* alters the way Americans view their country and their dream of opportunity,[55] and Dreiser's depiction of the city reveals the way Americans are to view their environment.

Another way the city heightens uncertainty about atmosphere in Dreiser's work is through its dual roles as the new harbinger of the American dream and as the stealthy culprit of social ills. In Dreiser's fiction, the city is both the place of opportunity and the place where people are lost to ambiguity. It is an environment that functions ambiguously as the new frontier of the American success dream and as the destroyer of those dreams. The city is a place that attracts with the promise of financial gain; however, it also relegates many of those it attracts to poverty and degradation.

Even though Dreiser's conception of the city exhibits both promising and disillusioning potentials, the weight of Dreiser's description of the city is negative. The flight to the cities in the latter part of the nineteenth century personifies culturally what urbanization tends to produce in fiction—"a regimentation and control of human events."[56] Thus, Dreiser's "characters do not merely work out their destinies in cities; they are largely the creatures of those cities,"[57] and the creature that Dreiser describes as the product of those cities is not an admirable sight. The effect of the city is loneliness and isolation—an ironic result in such a crowded space. Dreiser describes the terrible loneliness that he witnesses in the urban environment in an essay entitled, "The Loneliness of the City."

> One of the most painful results of modern congestion in cities, with the accompanying stress of labor to live, is the utter isolation and loneliness of heart forced upon the average individual. So exacting are the conditions under which we are compelled to work, so disturbing the show of pleasures and diversions we cannot obtain, that the normal satisfaction in normal wants is almost entirely destroyed. . . . [city dwellers] live in small, comfortably furnished and very convenient apartments, but they live alone. . . . You might live there a year, or ten years, and I doubt if your next-door neighbor would even so much as know of your existence. He is too busy. . . . It is all as if you really did not exist. . . . They are alone, left longing for a personal relationship, with an aching and, too often, a breaking heart. Friendship, affection, tenderness, how they loom large in the hour of despair![58]

In Dreiser's novels, the city is the setting where the American dream of success resides, yet the price of that dream is great. With the urbanization of America, we sacrifice human relationships and the ability to relate meaningfully to others. Urban America, as portrayed in Dreiser's work, is an ambiguous environment that creates uncertainties for its inhabitants. As such, the city exerts a powerful control over the lives of its inhabitants, and, while not fully deterministic, it appears as an otherness that retains and exercises power and awesomeness. Thus, the urban environment plays the role for Dreiser that the frontier plays for Cather. Both present themselves as otherness, and both impede the ability to relate meaningfully to others.

Because of his picture of the city, Dreiser may appear to be a Darwinian naturalist and a Spencerian socialist, but it is incorrect to say that he advocates a social world built upon these principles. Rather, he simply describes what he believes to be the forces that operate in society. The social world is cruel and operates in a way that leaves both winners and losers unhappy and dissatisfied. Thus, Lester dies with regrets and leaves a lonely Jennie behind; Hurstwood commits suicide and Carrie is an unfulfilled dreamer; Clyde is executed while Sondra loses her lover. Dreiser's response to the Darwinian world of his age results in a negative view of the social world and the people condemned to function in social space.

Dreiser responds to his time and helps to create the mood of his time with his fiction. On the one hand, he inherits the Darwinian worldview of his generation and the changing social scene of his country. Yet, on the other hand, his fiction itself uses this material and shapes it in a way to create and make sense of a world that people do not always understand. Dreiser's fictional world arises from deterministic philosophical materials, and in turn, it molds a setting that is divorced from sacred significance. Dreiser writes about a time that has removed the divine from the universe and that secularizes a traditionally sacred America. In religious and philosophical terms, his philosophy resembles Calvinistic determinism without God,[59] for in Dreiser's deterministic world, fate, chance, and the environment are sovereign and replace God.

Nevertheless, Dreiser's fiction does more than tear down the worldview of a century past (the romantic worldview) and expose the evils of the present ruling philosophy (the survival of the fittest). Dreiser's work contains a more positive pole of thought—a mode of thought that reappropriates the shattered American social dream in secularized and natural terms-a mode of thought that emphasizes the importance of individual relationships. The negative, disillusioning vision of his fiction finds its counterpart in a positive assessment of the role in human life of personal relationships—an assessment based on a pietistic naturalism.

4. Worldview Redefinition

PIETISTIC NATURALISM IN DREISER'S FICTION

Theodore Dreiser's fiction inherited and fostered a shift in the way Americans viewed their land and society. With the prevailing Darwinian and Spencerian approach to reality, the traditional romantic conception of supernatural presence in the world was no longer applicable. Furthermore, with the advent of Spencerian rules for society, the American dream of social and financial success was reduced to a system of injustice and hopelessness. However, although Dreiser's work describes this situation, Dreiser is not the strict determinist of "utter pessimism" as critics suggest. Rather, his insistent questioning and search for the truth result in a fiction that displays a pervasive hope in a reappropriation of the way Americans view their world and society.[60] This positive pole of Dreiserian naturalism coincides with the negative exorcism of the supernatural from the universe. This positive pole can be called a natural pietism—or pietistic naturalism.

David Brion Davis's essay, "Dreiser and Naturalism Revisited," is helpful in defining pietism and naturalism. Davis uses the traditional understanding of pietism and applies it to literature and art. Pietism is the rejection of traditional beliefs concerning the supernatural and the dependence upon existential experience in its place. Thus, a pietistic work of art is one in which the artist rejects long accepted ideas concerning God and nature and depends upon personal experience. Naturalism, for Davis, is defined as opposition to the supernatural. A naturalistic piece of literature is one in which the author rejects the presence of supernatural reality.[61]

If one combines the two concepts, pietistic naturalism emerges as a term that aptly describes the positive pole of Dreiser's fiction. Pietistic naturalism rejects the concept of God existing in nature in order to do justice to the personal experience of the natural itself. Thus, as with the negative pole of Dreiser's thought, the positive pole begins with contemplation of the natural world that ultimately holds consequences for social relationships. This development emerges most clearly in *The Bulwark*.

Lionel Trilling, Granville Hicks, and others tend to see *The Bulwark* as an inconsistency in Dreiser's philosophy. This is because they tend to associate Solon Barnes's unity with nature as an expression of pantheistic awe and, thus, with a sacred or "otherness oriented" conception of reality.[62] However, this is a misunderstanding of Dreiser's conception of nature in this work. Solon's peace at the end of the novel does not come through a sacred encounter with the divine in nature. Rather, his peace comes through Solon's discovery of natural reality itself and with the possibility of his relationship with it. Thus, Solon does not go to nature in order to experience the "other" that is beyond or within nature; rather, he goes to nature because he discovers the value, for him, that nature possesses in and of itself.

As a result, Dreiser's work represents a shift from the romantic emphasis on that which is "other than" nature, and it establishes a strong base for naturalistic philosophy by denying the supernatural presence in nature. In this same affirmation, Dreiser epitomizes a pietistic approach to nature because he denies a traditional understanding of God's presence in the world, and he affirms the untraditional emphasis on the unity of all reality. This understanding of the universe is possible in the latter nineteenth and early twentieth centuries because the Darwinian scientific worldview shatters traditional conceptions of the universe as it filters down to the popular mind. George Santayana comments on the piety of Theodore Dreiser and describes his pietistic naturalism.

"Philosophic piety . . . has the universe for its object. . . . Its extent, its order, its beauty, its cruelty, make it alike impressive. . . . Great is the organism of mud and fire, terrible this vast, painful, glorious experiment. Why should we not look on the universe with piety?"[63]

The Bulwark is not a capitulation to sentimental religion by a dying man; rather, it is the mature expression of a philosophical approach to life that appears throughout Dreiser's work. It is the final rejection of otherworldliness, and it issues a bold challenge to face life experientially. This notion—the expelling of the supernatural—extends itself from the natural realm into the social in the form of the great Quaker doctrine that Solon finally understands at the end of the novel. For Solon, the Inner Light is *not* something "other" that resides in human beings. One should not seek after the light only to neglect the receptacle. Rather, the Inner Light refers to the inherent goodness and worthiness of the person as a natural being—not as the medium for the manifestation of the supernatural. It follows that the requirement of the Inner Light is to honor and love all people.

Solon receives this revelation about the Inner Light shortly before his death, and the words in the introduction of John Woolman's *Journal* take on special meaning for him. "'His religion was love. His whole existence and all of his passions were love.'"[64] Etta notes the effect that these words have upon Solon, and she accurately senses the special unity with nature and with human beings that Solon discovers and that Dreiser's fiction describes.

In this love and unity with all nature, as she now sensed, there was nothing fitful or changing or disappointing—nothing that glowed one minute and was gone the next. This love was rather as constant as na-

ture itself, everywhere the same, in sunshine or in darkness, the filtered splendor of the dawn, the seeded beauty of the night. It was
an intimate relation to the very heart of being.[65]

This is the attitude that causes Dreiser's characters to turn their
search away from some supernatural object and toward an egalitarian principle that recognizes "the need of love toward all created things."[66]

Dreiser's work at this point shows a distinct Quaker influence.
In particular, this influence stems from Dreiser's correspondence
from 1938–1945 with Rufus Jones, an eminent Quaker historian
and mystic. So it is not surprising that Jones was "the greatest single influence on the final version of *The Bulwark*." In fact, Dreiser
gained his knowledge of Woolman's *Journal* by digesting Jones's
Finding the Trail of Life and *The Trial of Life in Middle Years*.[67] Gerhard Friedrich compares Dreiser's *The Bulwark* with Jones's writings and demonstrates that much of the plot of *The Bulwark*, and
some of its religious themes, closely parallel John Woolman's ideas
as recorded by Jones.

Friedrich speculates this is so because Dreiser owned, read, un-
derlined, and marked at least three of Jones's books. *Finding the
Trail of Life* especially influenced Dreiser's composition of *The Bulwark*. For example, according to Friedrich,

> Solon Barnes, the hero of *The Bulwark*, is modeled after Rufus Jones,
> but the name Rufus is transferred to Solon's father; Jones's mother
> and his Aunt Peace are blended into the character of Hannah
> Barnes, Solon's mother; and Jones's father is identified with Rufus
> Barnes. . . .[68]

Furthermore, the plot of *The Bulwark* closely resembles the life
pilgrimage of Rufus Jones. This is especially true in part 1. One
of the most important parallels recounts an ax wound that Solon
suffers—a wound that eventually leads to infection and to Solon's
discovery of the love and grace of God through his mother's care.
Jones describes a similar foot wound that leads to infection and
nearly kills him, and he credits this experience with changing his
life by learning of God's love through his Aunt Peace's care.[69]

Parallels to Jones's life occur throughout the first section of *The
Bulwark* even down to the likeness of personal traits between
Solon and Jones. Yet, perhaps the most important similarity
comes with Jones's contemplation of the problem of evil after an
antagonistic group burns down the Quaker meeting place.[70] The-

odicy proves to be Solon Barnes's path to discovery, and the problem of evil plagues and motivates other Dreiserian characters as well. Perhaps it is here that Dreiser first discovered his affinity for the Quaker religion.

Another important similarity between Jones's life and Dreiser's book occurs at the beginning of part 2 of the *The Bulwark* and involves the death of Solon's mother. This experience proves to be a test for Solon's faith. However, what is a small episode in the Jones experience feeds the thematic tensions that dominate Solon Barnes's struggle with faith and the question of theodicy.[71] Finally, Solon Barnes's death-bed comfort from John Woolman's *Journal* reflects Dreiser's own exposure to and impression of Woolman's writings as made available through his friend, Rufus Jones.[72]

Nevertheless, with all of Dreiser's close and intimate association with the Friends and with Jones, Quaker reviewers of *The Bulwark* are quick to express their disapproval of Dreiser's representation of their religion. One Quaker reviewer begins his treatment of *The Bulwark* with the following statement: "Friends will read this book with strong to violent disapproval." This is because Dreiser's understanding of the Inner Light is not the traditional Quaker expression of this central doctrine.[73] Dreiser subtly reinterprets the central teaching of the Quaker religion. The Inner Light for Quakers represents a part of the divine in human beings—a supernatural spark within the person. However, in *The Bulwark*, the Inner Light refers to the worthiness of humanity without the need of the divine spark—human beings are worthy in and of themselves. Therefore, Dreiser's understanding of the Inner Light does not allow "a sound basis for a religious society" as the Quaker view of it does.[74] Rather, Dreiser's view helps to reinforce his contention that God does not operate in society and that humanity must reconcile itself to the inherent goodness of human beings without the illusions that they are participating in divine nature.

Dreiser expresses this thought as he responds to Rufus Jones's belief in "'opening ourselves to God's influence' [and becoming] . . . the organ of a divine purpose." As Dreiser read this, he penciled in the margin of Jones's work, "It is the other way around. Nature opens us to her influences."[75] Dreiser cannot accept God working in human beings or in society. Rather, human beings are good because they are infused and part of the natural realm—not the supernatural. Dreiser's characters' experience of unity with the natural realm appears in his novels in contrast to the deca-

dence of the unnatural as well as to the supernatural. The automobile and the city are two prime representatives of that which
is antagonistic to the nobility of the natural,[76] but equally so is the
insistence of imposing supernatural legitimation upon the natural
realm. For Dreiser, the supernatural is an unnatural and artificial
intrusion upon natural unity.

Furthermore, this philosophy of unity rejects the Darwinian description of hostile forces in nature; rather, what appears as ruthless in a Darwinian world is but the expression of a natural
harmony independent of any supernatural sponsorship or moral
guidelines. For example, as Solon enjoys his first walk through the
garden near the end of *The Bulwark,* he observes a fly eating a
flower. This passage recalls the lobster and squid passage in *The
Financier;* however, whereas the lobster and squid passage presents a ruthless view of a Darwinian world ruled by the survival
of the fittest, this passage appears as a celebration of the world's
natural beauty and harmony. Nature still operates by the Darwinian principle, but Solon is able to understand this without despair
or ruthless instinct. Rather, he recognizes the worth and the nobility of the natural process.

It is this return to the natural realm and its beauty that allows
Dreiser to reformulate a vision of society in response to the ruthless social order that surrounds him. In Dreiser's fiction, the order
which society should reveal does not derive from God's ruling the
world; nor does natural order derive from God's control of natural events. However, order is imparted to the world by a deistic
creator God, and order resides in the natural world itself.[77] God
is not in this world, although the deity started it all. Since the
order implanted by this creator is to be seen more in nature than
in society, modern human beings experience a conflict between
their nature as created beings and their existence as social beings.

Dreiser advocates, therefore, a social space consistent with natural space, and he creates a new social paradigm to replace the
ruthless, competitive social world that he abhors. In Dreiser's fiction, social reality mirrors natural laws; therefore, social theory
derives from meditation upon the natural world. The same is true
with this positive pole of Dreiser's pietistic naturalism as applied
to the social world. The harmony that occurs in nature without
the supernatural can also exist in society without the transcendent.

Two examples from Dreiser's fiction illustrate this development
from natural harmony to models of social order. First, Eugene
Witla, Dreiser's autobiographical character from *The "Genius",* ex-

periences "harmony with the universe" and escapes the shackles of society with his realization and acceptance of an evolutionary universe with God as creator of but absent from the world.

> It is very necessary to presuppose some vast intelligence, some pervading spirit, to explain the guidance of the lower forces in accordance with the preordained system of evolution we see prevailing. . . . The infinitely varied products of the animal and vegetable kingdoms [are] . . . a preparation for ourselves, to assist in our mental development, and to fit us for a progressively higher state of existence. . . .[78]

Witla recognizes that a God created the world and set in motion natural and evolutionary processes that rule the natural world. And even though that God is no longer present in the world, a divinely derived order resides in nature and can be extended to the social world.

However, the clearest example of the move from natural to social harmony in Dreiser's fiction comes from *The Bulwark.* Solon finds this truth during his second walk in the garden. When the puff adder moves across his foot without biting, he realizes that the created order strives simply for "good intent."[79] Love, unity, and goodwill are the lessons that Solon learns from nature. These lessons give him the key to what personal relationships can be and to how society should be ordered.

> I do not think the world quite realizes what . . . essential element[s] the affections and . . . tenderness really are. . . . We cannot do without . . . [relationships]. After all is said and done, we must truly love one another or we must die—alone, neglected, despised and forgotten, as too many of us die.[80]

The lesson of nature—the lesson of "good intent"—is the only lesson that can infuse the ruthless social world with harmony and with order.

Dreiser extends this lesson of good intent and unity from Quakerism to Hinduism and to his own beliefs.[81] In *The Stoic,* Berenice naturally turns to Hinduism in order to find peace after Cowperwood's death. Like Solon, she finds peace through a philosophy of unity—the Hindu philosophy of the unity of existence, and she discovers that the answer to life comes in the form of selfless love to others. Berenice realizes that

> her entire life . . . with the exception of the past few years—had been

spent in the pursuit of pleasure and self-advancement. But now she knew that one must live for something outside of one's self, something that would tend to answer the needs of the many as opposed to the vanities and comforts of the few, of which she herself was one. What could she do to help?[82]

Berenice and Solon discover the need of true love that contradicts the "I satisfy myself" philosophy of so many Dreiserian characters. Therefore, with the positive pole in Dreiser's fictional environment, the reader finds not only the exorcism of the supernatural from the world, but also a rejection of the individualistic rule of life that tends to evolve from the Darwinian and Spencerian world of self advancement. This is possible when one focuses on immanent reality rather than upon transcendent possibility, for only in the immanent moment does one experience true love of humanity.

This loss of the transcendent may at first seem to destroy otherness and religious meaning. It seems akin to a "death of God" scenario wherein ultimacy disappears leaving a mundane or profane existence bereft of meaning or moral and spiritual potentiality. However, this is not the case. In Dreiser's fiction, as also in Cather's, otherness is not destroyed because otherness is necessary for a well-integrated human existence. Rather, otherness is rediscovered. For Cather, the physical landscape is ultimately ambiguous and mysterious, and the land itself replaces the transcendent as otherness. In Dreiser's fiction, both nature and the city (the social world) appear shrouded in ambiguity. The natural and the social realms both transcend the human capacity to understand, predict, or control. Therefore, in Dreiser's work, the natural realm and the social realm, which are both divested of supernatural presence, present themselves as ultimate reality or as otherness.

The otherness of atmosphere (especially the social world) controls human life in Dreiser's fiction. This is a drastic shift from the romantic conception of a world controlled by the transcendent—this is the secularization of American space. However, secularization is not equivalent to lack of faith; rather, it exchanges one orientation of American space (the sacred view) for another (the secular view) and develops a third, reconstituted religious affirmation of space. In Dreiser's fiction, the new otherness is a nature that can direct and correct a social order based on mutual respect and love—a social order that holds a reverence for the anthropological rather than the supernatural. The religious devotion to this quotidian reality finds expression in acts of selfless love toward others. In other words, the ontological beliefs embedded in Dreiser's fiction produce a system of social and personal ethics.

AN ETHIC OF HUMANITARIAN MORALITY

Many critics suggest that Dreiser rejects morality because he destroys the traditional ideas concerning moral right and wrong. These critics understand Dreiser's conception of life as completely void of meaning or value.[83] This conclusion arises if one only focuses upon the negative pole of Dreiser's naturalism; however, Dreiser's naturalism is ambiguous, and his moral code is not so obvious. Nevertheless, moral principle is not absent from Dreiser's work.[84] He rejects traditional ideas of morality; his ethical and philosophical ideas demonstrate ambiguity, and they waver between two poles; yet, Dreiser's work is moral from the core—it arises from moral concerns and from the inability of traditional morality to function in his secularized urban space. Theodore Dreiser rejects conventional morality in order to reveal a new ethic based upon humanitarian concern rather than upon supernatural righteousness.

Moral truth for Dreiser disguises itself and contains the "bewildering faculty of the chameleon."[85] Dreiser's urban society is secularized, pluralistic, and complex, and it no longer exhibits the homogeneity that characterizes much of early nineteenth-century America—it can no longer claim a single religious or moral viewpoint. This is the beginning of his heightened moral code. In Dreiser's fiction, his new morality depends directly upon the changing and secularizing social space. With the rise of religious and cultural pluralism, traditional cultural standards of right and wrong are no longer unified or certain. Thus, Dreiser's so-called moral rejection liberates a vast number of Americans who find themselves ostracized from the privileged stream of social acceptability. "Dreiser's work is of such importance . . . because he renders for us this world of fantastic incertitude;"[86] no set standards of right and wrong exist for Dreiser. When people try to impose a set standard, the result is the oppression of many who cannot live by such a code.

Dreiser's ambiguous moral code, which arises in response to his developing secularized social setting, appears throughout his novels. He experienced a major interruption in writing *Sister Carrie* at the point that Hurstwood examines money from an open safe at his place of employment; Dreiser's problem was to have Hurst-

wood take the money without appearing guilty. Thus, the door
to the safe mysteriously closes, and Hurstwood panics and leaves
with the money. Dreiser at least wants the reader to ponder
Hurstwood's guilt or innocence. This same dilemma occurs to a
greater extent in *An American Tragedy.* Clyde plots Roberta's mur-
der by drowning, yet he has a change of heart at the last minute.
Then Clyde, frustrated and confused, strikes Roberta acciden-
tally, the boat capsizes, and Clyde watches Roberta drown as he
swims safely to shore. It is an accident, but is he guilty? He swims
away without attempting to save her, and it is clear that he is an
excellent swimmer who could have easily saved a drowning victim. And what about all the planning that Clyde schemes in order
to carry out just such an event? Does his last minute change of
heart really absolve him from guilt? Dreiser purposely creates a
moral ambiguity to demonstrate that set standards for right and
wrong are too simplistic for the complexities of human feelings
and relationships. Traditional moral categories are only adequate
for the "stupid and lethargic."[87]

The uselessness of traditional, conventional moral codes, in an
increasingly pluralistic and secular social world, appears as a
major theme in Dreiser's novels. These codes spark rebellion in
the younger generation because they are outdated and inadequate. Thus, when Dreiser writes a book like *Sister Carrie,* it is not
surprising that it appears as offensive; Dreiser's system of morality strikes directly at the genteel tradition and renders it invalid.[88]
Carrie's Victorian virtue no longer counts, and she is not pun-
ished for what the convention of Dreiser's day abhors. In this
sense, Dreiser's fiction is subversive, for it attacks the prevailing
system of morality of his time.

Dreiser's unrelenting attack upon this system of morality stems
from his own harsh encounter with stifling moral codes. These
codes arise from inherited religious beliefs and from the American social dream of success. Much of Dreiser's writing depicts conservative religious characters who mirror scenes from Dreiser's
encounters with his father's religious beliefs and with his exposure to the religious legerdemain performed by fanatics such as
Asa Conklin (the real life counterpart to Asa Griffiths).[89] Religion,
for Dreiser, appears as "an illusion capable of deceiving only
those blind to life's realities."[90] In *An American Tragedy,* fundamental and evangelical religion operates as a "cloudy romance" that
has nothing to do with life. It is based on guilt, and it infects like
a "virus." Inherited social mores and religious beliefs construct artificial taboos that prevent the weak from aspiring to greater

heights. Furthermore, the fundamentalist attitude toward religion is little more than an escape for Dreiser, because it focuses so much on otherworldly reality in order to avoid dealing with present reality.[91] Thus, traditional religion appears incapable of preparing one for life in Dreiser's complex social world. This is especially true in the case of Clyde Griffiths.

While considering Clyde, one can isolate the true American tragedy; it occurs in a world where opportunity for advancement abounds and where moral and religious codes exist to stifle one's ability to make progress—where the social dreams conflict with the social rules. In Dreiser's America, the codes that restrict progress emerge from the conception of the social world that fundamentalist religion refuses to compromise. This mythopoeic worldview appears in light of the biblical creation story and presupposes God's loving presence in society. Dreiser cannot accept this conception of the world because it does not adequately deal with the problem of evil. Dreiser's fundamentalist has no sensitivity to human suffering because he focuses upon otherness to the extent that he loses sight of the "thisness" of the world; as a result, the fundamentalist view of reality in Dreiser's work denies more than it affirms and damages more than it protects or heals. Therefore, the need for a revised morality is apparent for Dreiser, because America must confront a revised understanding of social space.

Clyde Griffiths is exemplary of this notion. For example, Clyde's inability to cope with the world stems directly from his immersion in the otherworldly view of reality that his parents espouse. Clyde's mother begins to realize the failure of this view of the world toward the end of the book. She reminisces about Clyde, and she thinks that his strict religious upbringing may be partly to blame for his downfall. Then she turns to Russell (Clyde's sister's illegitimate child) and realizes that something must change.

> Her darling boy. The light and color of her declining years. She must be kind to him, more liberal with him, not restrain him too much, as maybe, maybe, she had—She looked affectionately and yet a little vacantly after him as he ran. 'For *his* sake.'[92]

The italicized emphasis upon *his* (for Russell's sake), which occurs in a formulaic expression of prayer (for his sake), indicates that Clyde's mother finally realizes that moral codes should benefit human beings rather than some abstract conception of what religionists believe to be righteous acts before God.

Thus, for Dreiser, the inherited religious tradition and its conventional morality emanate from a sacred understanding of social space and stand in opposition to the development of humanity in a secular, social world. In addition, the Darwinian world creates an environment that stifles the hope of the masses. However, Dreiser's fiction does not leave its readers in despair. Rather, a higher concept of morality emerges from the positive pole of Dreiser's naturalistic philosophy. His conception of morality appears in at least two forms. The first manifestation of this ethical principle occurs in what Donald Pizer terms the aesthetic approach to moral judgment. This mode of moral judgment actualizes the libertine desire of the human spirit; it occurs in Cowperwood who collects art and beautiful women in his search for aesthetic perfection; it appears as the main theme in Dreiser's most autobiographical novel, The "Genius", when Eugene Witla epitomizes the artistic, libertine impulse as he exercises his need "to be free to pursue beauty."[93] The second form of Dreiser's morality appears in characters like Jennie Gerhardt who are free enough to blaze their own humanistic system of morality. Therefore, the prerequisite of Dreiser's higher morality is freedom from conventional views of right and wrong. Yet, only the "visionary" character escapes the stifling bounds of social conventionality and is able to realize a higher religious ideal and moral principle.[94] Only those characters like Jennie Gerhardt, who courageously step beyond the social boundaries set by convention, discover true virtue and morality. Only those characters with vision escape the societal competition for survival and discover a code for life that brings peace. What is this higher morality that Dreiser calls virtue? Virtue is the life that Jennie epitomizes.

> Virtue is that quality of generosity which offers itself willingly for another's service, and, being this, it is held by society to be nearly worthless. . . . Jennie had not sought to hold herself dear. Innate feeling in her made for self-sacrifice.[95]

Thus, Jennie cares more for others than she does for herself and gives of herself sacrificially. For this she accepts disapproval by the codes and standards of society. Nevertheless, for Dreiser, "morality is always larger than the explicit codes through which men say they rule their actions, and life larger than its codes and rules."[96]

5. Summary

Theodore Dreiser was caught between worlds as America's symbols experienced a critical transformation. His life and the lives he witnessed around him were in turmoil—they were destined to relentless ambiguity. To explain this ambiguous existence, Dreiser wavered between two conflicting worldviews (the sacred romantic worldview and the scientific Darwinian worldview), and in the end, neither was sufficient to set his mind at peace. Rather, the world in Dreiser's fiction is like Cather's in that it denies both the sacrality of the romantic world and the determinism of Darwin's world. Furthermore, like Cather, in Dreiser's fiction, there is no otherness beyond this world; rather, the environment appears as ultimate and as otherness. Whereas in Cather's fiction the frontier (natural space) appears as otherness, in Dreiser's fiction, the city (social space) takes on the characteristics of otherness. For example, the city attracts people to it, yet it also destroys many who answer its beckoning call. Thus, the city is powerful, ambiguous, and mysterious—in short, the city is "other."

As a result of this new designation of otherness, there is no transcendent reality beyond one's environment, and Dreiser's characters must depend on one another in order to face the uncertainty of existence that results from living in an ambiguous and mysterious world. Ultimately, Dreiser's fiction suggests a new moral code that is based upon natural worth—a code that replaces the traditional code of ethics that is based upon otherworldly sovereignty. Dreiser's moral code not only belittles the narcissistic nature of society and ruthless human beings, but it also suggests a higher moral code and ethical system that replaces the inadequate nature of traditional religion. Solon Barnes discovers the true ethical principle in the writings of John Woolman. A true religion is not "limited by society or creed . . . [or] narrow morality." Rather, a true moral system is one that aids people to "become brethren."[97]

Dreiser rejects the romantic worldview of divine otherness contained in the world because he sees no evidence of God's control either over nature or over society. Rather, society and nature appear controlled by the forces of a Darwinian universe, and human beings experience estrangement from their familiar and comfortable conception of a sacred world. When they turn to the social environment for meaning, they encounter a ruthless world of survival and competition. However, some of Dreiser's characters find peace in this social world through observation of the natural realm whence they learn that human beings must turn to one another with good intent and love sacrificially. Dreiser's morality is based upon humanitarian love—love for the sake of the person and not for the sake of divine benefits. For Dreiser, this humanitarian moral principle is the only comfort we have as we face the threat of life—Jennie's lonely curse of "days and days in endless reiteration."[98]

4

A New American Dream

Dislocation as Reminiscent of a Century Past and Reorientation as Prophetic of the Modern World

This final chapter moves from the specific to the general. What begins as a narrow concern for America at the time of Willa Cather and Theodore Dreiser informs the broader continuing story of American life in the twentieth century as the same patterns emerge to solidify American cultural history. These patterns, in turn, spawn a general concern for the whole religion and culture question; they summarize and augment the main arguments of this study, but they also address a more specific question—"How does the process of secularization in America reflect the cultural dynamics present in the broader relationship of religion to literature?"

1. Dislocation and Reappropriation

I have attempted to isolate a pattern that describes both religious and cultural trends in the latter nineteenth and early twentieth centuries. This pattern involves questioning accepted tenets, rejecting them, and ultimately redefining them in light of new and changing cultural and social circumstances so that they make sense. This pattern depends upon self-critique and moves one from a situation of uncertainty to an experience of wholeness. The *fin de siècle* American experienced such a situation of uncertainty and was dislocated from the familiar world. Thus, the dynamics that defined turn-of-the-century literature and religion revolve around a concept of dislocation and marginality, and they evolve as the search for resolution occurs.

The concepts of dislocation and reappropriation constitute a pattern and are used in this study in three ways. The first way lo-

111

cates historical trends and the characterization of these trends in the fiction of the time. This pattern describes the experience of Americans in the nineteenth and early twentieth centuries—they had lost their familiar world and were searching for legitimacy in a new, meaningful environment. However, not only does this pattern describe the experience of historical America, it also describes the characterization of fictional America. In the fiction of Cather and Dreiser, the movement from dislocation to reappropriation grows from the relationship between character and atmosphere; many of their characters are peripheral and seek centrality, dislocated and seek reorientation. As such they are representative of Americans at the end of the nineteenth century.

Second, this process describes an hermeneutical principle that allows the search for truth within a text. A narrative text makes expanded worlds of possibility available to the reader through the presentation of atmosphere,[1] and this larger world acts to challenge the adequacy of the reader's smaller, restricted world. This challenge throws the reader's accepted notions of truth into question and holds open new possibilities; it removes a familiar and accepted notion from its position of centrality and replaces it with new possibilities of meaning. Nevertheless, the process of dislocation is not only negative—it not only questions one system of truth. Rather, the hermeneutical principle of questioning accepted notions and redefining them opens up new worlds of meaning, and interpretation occurs when the world of the interpreter and the world of the text merge to produce a more complete world of meaning.[2]

Finally, the third way that I use the process of dislocation and reappropriation is to describe cultural and religious dynamics and their interaction with one another. The movement from dislocation to location—from a position of illegitimacy to one of legitimacy—describes the social and cultural forces that are incipient not only in literature but in religion and other cultural forms as well. Such a theory presents a comprehensive view of culture from which one can decipher the relationship between religion and literature. With these three uses of these terms in mind, it is now possible to turn to an examination of how these dynamics operated in the historical and fictional world of the late nineteenth and early twentieth centuries in America.

2. Transition in America: The Story of Willa Cather and Theodore Dreiser And the Realistic Redefinition of America

I use the fiction and the cultural situation of nineteenth-century America to highlight this movement from dislocation to reorientation, because it demonstrates the American quest for wholeness. This quest took place in the nineteenth century through the exchange of one worldview for another; cultural transitions participated in questioning and rejecting a sacred worldview and in redefining the world in secular terms. In other words, the nineteenth century and the early twentieth century witnessed the death of sacred America and the birth of a secularized society. The end result of the secularization of America was the creation of an alien environment for which turn-of-the-century Americans were not ready. These Americans were precariously situated between the comfortable agrarian world of their roots and the industrial modern world of anonymity. Americans were removed from their familiar world and became outsiders or "estrangers."[3]

This sacred world that was lost appears in many different guises in many different studies of American religion and culture; I choose to envision this sacred world in the context of the American dream of possibility. From the beginnings of America, a complex system of civil religion matured in order to describe a land founded upon the dream of possibility and opportunity. The reason that this country offers such opportunity, according to the creed of this civil religion, is because God smiles upon America—the chosen nation, which God will continue to bless, as long as Americans continue to do the will of God. Thus, opportunity in this land, as defined by American civil religion, is dependent upon God's continued presence in the land.[4]

In the early part of the nineteenth century these notions filtered through the romantic tradition and emerged as a bipolar expression of the American sacred vision. On the one hand, God is contained in nature, and the physical world of America is sacred. On the other hand, God dwells in human beings, and the social world of men and women is sacred. When this is combined with the American dream of possibility, sacred America is defined in two different ways; the frontier describes the natural pole of the sacred American dream while the emerging city represents the social pole of the sacred vision of America. Both of these visions of America were challenged during the nineteenth century, and the result was the secularization of both physical and social American space, which is in turn a reappropriation of the American dream. Such a redefinition was brought about by the challenge that dislocation brought to the nineteenth-century American through the intrusion of Darwinism, through the transition from rural countryside to city slum, and through the invasion of the foreign immigrant.

The experience of dislocation and alienation altered cultural and religious forms and experiences in the latter nineteenth and early twentieth centuries. Religious and literary expression are both existential quests for ontological wholeness—quests initiated by ontological estrangement or dislocation. The assumption behind this model is that religion and literature are not formed in the abstract and handed down from theologians and artists; rather, they arise from life and in turn, help make it possible. Furthermore, dislocation and reorientation are the conceptual categories that inform the hermeneutical model used here to examine the fiction of Cather and Dreiser. For Cather, Americans are alienated from their natural surroundings, and for Dreiser people are isolated from social familiarity and exposed to Darwinian forces that govern social relationships.

Nevertheless, no work on Cather or Dreiser can claim legitimacy if it only focuses upon the negative and the destructive effects of dislocation. While cultural dislocation in the latter nineteenth century led to religious and social alienation, this alienation led to rethinking and reappropriating the American dream and ultimately to enriching cultural forms. The same is true with the fiction of Cather and Dreiser. In fact, the pessimism that often pervades their work contains an underlying kernel of optimism and the belief in something that can be better.[5] Cather destroys the American dream concerning natural space, but she reappropriates the dream in terms of social space. Thus, where the hostile physical environment crushes one, heightened human relationships rescue one from alienation. Conversely, Dreiser destroys the American dream concerning social space, yet he redefines the dream in terms of the natural world. Where God no longer operates within society, personal wholeness can only be experienced in a totally natural world—a world stripped of the supernatural. Yet, in the end, Dreiser's fiction extends this lesson from the natural world to the social world in order to form a new social vision based on (like Cather) heightened interpersonal relationships.

The result of this process of rejection and redefinition is a new

American vision that posits a secularized vision of American physical and social space—a vision that relies upon relating to persons and to the environment without the sacred qualifications imposed upon them by the romantic poets. Thus, while Cather and Dreiser complete the secularization of physical and social American space by desacralizing the natural world and by destroying conventional social order, their act is prophetic of and prepares for the modern explosion of literature to follow. Furthermore, this act is one of positive world appropriation that results from dislocation and the search for legitimation.

One purpose of this study is the examination of Cather and Dreiser in the context of their cultural milieu as they participate in the pattern of rejection and redefinition. In their search, both Cather and Dreiser hail the necessity of human relationships, and they desacralize the universe so that the full value of nature and human relationships can emerge. Their work reveals a similar three-stage process; however, they find their answers in different places. The stages that the fiction of Cather and Dreiser reflect are: (1) dislocation/isolation; (2) search for constancy; and (3) reappropriation/resolution/harmony. For Cather, isolation occurs on the frontier in the natural realm while for Dreiser dislocation takes place in the context of the city or social world. Cather's fiction participates in the search for constancy by finding peace in social relationships while Dreiser finds his peace in the natural realm. However, these reversals both find resolution and harmony in the form of heightened interpersonal relationships.

Nevertheless, through focusing on Cather and Dreiser in this work and through this summary, I do not suggest that these were the only two writers in the nineteenth and twentieth centuries who participated in the pattern of dislocation to reappropriation. Rather, most of the major works of the time followed this same pattern. In fact, the realistic tradition, which blossomed at this time, fostered the pattern of dislocation to reappropriation through its focus on the effects of environment on character. This focus promoted the type of questioning and search that spawned Cather's and Dreiser's fiction. In different ways and to varying degrees, the authors of realistic works in the late nineteenth and early twentieth centuries struggled with similar quests for meaning and with the reappropriation of a failing worldview that dominated the fiction of Willa Cather and Theodore Dreiser.

One of the first steps in the realistic redefinition of American space involves a restatement of the romantic concept of the natural world as sacred realm. Nature is still the realm in which

human beings find spiritual integrity; however, in the realistic restatement, the natural realm is no longer seen as benevolent, and
spiritual communion with nature is not always expressed in peaceful or positive terms. Furthermore, this sacred natural realm is
often defined over against the social world that appears as perverse. In this realistic restatement, the world of people is stifling
and spiritually retarding, and one can find redemptive value only
in the world of nature that is irreconcilable with the social world.

This concept is a subtle shift from the romantic tradition in
which the social world can be redeemed by participation in the
natural realm, and it supports only the sacred natural pole of the
bipolar American dream of possibility. But even the view of nature shifts in this restatement of the sacred theme. Although the
world of nature still retains some of its sacred and redemptive
value, in this realistic restatement the world of nature is no longer
benevolent as it is in the romantic tradition. This first step in the
secularization of American space, thus, redefines the sacred character of *natural* space and grimly characterizes the social realm.
Kate Chopin's *The Awakening* and Mark Twain's *Adventures of
Huckleberry Finn* illustrate this redefinition of sacred American
space.[6]

Like Cather's fiction, Chopin's and Twain's works contrast a
perverse social world with a redeeming natural world. Thus, they
challenge the romantic notion that the social world is sacred.
However, even though nature maintains redeeming qualities,
they also refuse to accept the romantic notion of a benevolent and
sacred natural world that is a gateway to the transcendent. They
criticize the social world and strip society of its sacred qualities,
and they recast the natural world in a realistic yet favorable light.
This challenge to the familiar, benevolent natural environment
created a crisis for *fin de siècle* Americans who were losing their
claim on the disappearing natural landscape, and it replaced their
loss with a natural world that isolated rather than fulfilled. Nevertheless, in this realistic restatement of the romantic concept of environment, harmony with the natural realm provides the key to
personal fulfillment and integration. The discovery of such
wholeness occurs in the fiction of writers like Cather, Chopin, and
Twain when characters who lose the sacred, natural world reap-
propriate a familiar and harmonious environment where human
relationships can thrive.

On the opposite end of the spectrum, other realistic and naturalistic writers wrote about characters who were estranged from
the romantic notion of the *social* world. Along with Dreiser,

works like Stephen Crane's *The Red Badge of Courage* and Edith Wharton's *Ethan Frome* illustrate this characteristic of realistic literature.[7] In these works the social environment is questioned and the sacred social world of the romantics is rejected and redefined. Improper social relationships prove to be antithetical and restricting to the American dream of possibility. Instead of the redeeming social world of the romantic tradition, this realistic social world ironically creates isolation. Yet, even though the romantic view of the social world was insufficient and lost, a reappropriated view of social relationships became crucial to personal fulfillment and wholeness for these writers.

Throughout the nineteenth century, writers struggled with the bipolar sacred American dream that was in disrepair because of changing cultural and social conditions. Mark Twain and Kate Chopin continued to depict a desacralized nature as positive while rejecting the notion that society contained redeeming qualities. On the other hand, writers like Stephen Crane and Edith Wharton rejected the notion that nature was the key to wholeness and pictured the world of men and women as the place of meaning. Willa Cather and Theodore Dreiser struggled with the same issues as did many of the realistic and naturalistic writers of the nineteenth century and early twentieth century.

The result of all this was a redefinition of American natural and social space from a sacred and utopian garden to a secular and impersonal nation. Nevertheless, this new secular stance toward America does not imply a stance that is irreligious; rather, this new worldview has important religious qualities. It still implies an American dream, but the new American vision is a very different one than the one that had passed before and that was based upon a sacred and otherworldly stance to the world. This new vision of a "thisworldly" relation to America arose out of the experience of dislocation and led to a new experience of wholeness. Because it moved from disorientation to legitimacy, it is religious to the core—it provided meaning and truth to a people who were searching for meaning and orientation in a world that had been turned upside down.

* * *

I have described two different worldviews that dominated the American struggle for identity during the nineteenth century and early twentieth century and the transition from the one to the other. This is important for several reasons. First, sacred and secular models of America still exist at odds with one another in the present. By examining the struggles of the past to define America, one can better understand conflicting worldviews that inform the cultural, religious, and political scenes of the present. Second, the sacred and secular approach to the world may be at odds; however, it is wrong to assume that the former is religious while the latter is atheistic. They both represent ontologically and religiously important explanations of the world that provide meaning and wholeness. The realization of this fact lends a more complete understanding of the dynamics of the nineteenth century and of the present struggle to define America as a sacred or secular land. Third, the process of transition (acceptance—doubt—redefinition) from one worldview to another is in itself a religious exercise. This process moves one from disorientation to wholeness, or from doubt to belief, and, thus, parallels the religious search for truth. Therefore, the whole process of national definition is a religious exercise of self understanding on a grand scale. Finally, this examination of worldview redefinition through a literary medium necessarily offers implications for the relationship and the study of religion and literature. The model of dislocation-reappropriation establishes an intimate link between the belief structure incipient in literature and operative in religion. I will examine briefly these first two points in part 3, by more carefully defining the difference between sacred and secular, and I will develop the last two points in part 4, through an examination of narrative and religious theory.

3. Sacred and Secular—Apprehension and Reality: The Conflict of Two Religious Worlds in America

"REALITY OUTRAN APPREHENSION"

The romantic search for the divine in the cosmos recalls the classical distinction between sacred and secular conceptualizations of the world. When Giles Gunn speaks about romantic literature, he categorizes it using a sacred-secular polarization. Sacred and secular do not specify "different kinds of objects;" rather, these concepts refer to "different ways of perceiving and then relating ourselves to" the world. In speaking about *Moby Dick*, Gunn recounts its similarity to the transcendentalist view of nature. *Moby Dick*, the transcendentalists, and the romantic tradition in general approach nature and human beings as the receptacles of the divine—as the shrouds for otherness.[8]

The terms sacred and secular conjure many images and meanings, and it is thus necessary to define their origins more precisely.

The basis for understanding a sacred approach to environment arises from the definition of "sacred" and "profane" in the history of religions approach to religious traditions. Mircea Eliade elaborates upon Rudolf Otto's terminology and posits space as sacred when "manifestation of something of a wholly different order . . . [occurs] in objects that are an integral part of our natural 'profane' world."[9] Thus, a world is sacred when it possesses the ability to disclose the "other;" consequently, a secular world does not possess the ability to house the transcendent. Nevertheless, a secular world is not a world without religion, and secularity is not an invalidation of religion. Rather, it is an opposition to the sacred idea that there is ultimate reality beyond this world. For the sacred worldview, ultimate reality is beyond this world, while for the secular worldview, ultimate reality is this world. However, both stances to the world posit ultimate reality, and both are religious in that they imply ontological status—"two modes of being in the world."[10]

Lynn Ross-Bryant builds upon this secular-sacred dichotomy in her work, *Imagination and the Life of the Spirit.* Ross-Bryant traces the use of sacred terminology through the history of religions approach and affirms that the modern world is victim to a polarization of sacred attitudes and secular life. She uses Langdon Gilkey to assert the difference in sacred and secular approaches to life— the secular attitude being the "attitude of our time . . . that emphasizes the human rather than the transcendent."[11]

That "the romantic poets" presuppose "the presence of God within the object" and the reality of "supernatural power deeply interfused in nature" is not a startling supposition to contribute.[12] Nevertheless, the sacred world model is helpful in the attempt to chronicle the shift from romanticism to realism in American literature in the nineteenth century. The changing conception of the world in the nineteenth century reflects the human struggle to gain ontological status in relation to otherness. Thus, where the romantic poets find supernatural reality disclosed in nature and human beings, the realists must struggle with a new conceptual base after the rise of mid-century nihilism.[13] As a result, the sacred view of a world that points beyond the world to some greater reality is replaced in realism by either the conception of a world void of any greater reality or by a world that is synonymous with otherness (ultimate reality).

In the redefinition of American space from sacred to secular, this expulsion of supernatural reality appears as the operative force in much of the fiction that participated in the realistic and naturalistic traditions. In the fiction that reappropriated the romantic, sacred version of the world, the reality of the situation outruns the imagined quest for otherness—the otherness of this world is ultimate reality rather than the transcendence of worlds elsewhere. A final comparison between these sacred and secular worldviews emerges in Ishmael's encounter with Ahab in *Moby Dick*.

For days Ishmael pondered the queer warnings of old Elijah and tried to muster an image of the diabolical and mysterious Ahab. The Pequod was already several days out to sea. Where was this Ahab, and why had he not yet emerged from his shrouded retreat below? Such thoughts lurked in the mind of Ishmael until they boiled into a frenzy of expectancy. Yet, although the half-witted prophet, Elijah, predicted the unknown worst and the apparition of a mad demon, Ishmael was ill prepared for the appearance of Captain Ahab upon the quarter-deck of the Pequod. "Reality outran apprehension;" no amount of borrowed description or imagined expectation could adequately forewarn Ishmael of the reality of Ahab in the flesh. There he stood wilder than the mind's wildest imaginations.

Why is this appearance of Ahab so important to *Moby Dick* and to the romantic world of the nineteenth century? Ishmael's revelation on the quarter-deck of the Pequod is extraordinary in that it is radically different from the mundane experience of life that characterizes the greater part of human existence. In the ordinary course of events, one is usually disappointed by reality because apprehension and expectation are so great. Events are boring because they cannot match the mind's fantasia concerning life. Yet, Ishmael's experience of Ahab is different. He is so oriented to the lived experience that no amount of thought beforehand will spoil the daily encounter with reality. But what is it about this orientation to life that packs Ishmael's experience of reality with so much excitement and wonder? The appearance of Ahab as theophany serves as a model to delineate the differences between a romantic orientation to life, which is lost to the wonder of something beyond life, and Ishmael's approach to life, which allows a fresh and exhilarating step into the unknown realities of this world.

This difference of orientation to the world highlights the tensions between the sacred approach to the world and a secular one. Furthermore, from a comparison of these approaches to life, one might even argue that the secular worldview not only constitutes a religious stance to the world but that it is also a fully authentic way of being religious in the world, even when compared to the romantic or sacred worldviews. When one is consumed by the sacred approach to reality, one is constantly looking beyond forms in the search for essences, beyond the reality of human beings and nature in the search of something more. One possible result is that the sacred worldview directs energy beyond a meaningful encounter with the world toward an otherworldly preoccupation. Those oriented to the otherworldly may miss much of life because of an overriding drive to find that which is beyond life. The human result of this worldview, as characterized by Cather's and Dreiser's novels, is people who are maladjusted to deal with the complexity of life. Rather, they seek escape from problems and joys of the world in favor of protection within the folds of a promise of another world that is somehow beyond and better than this world. Although this stance seeks to provide fulfillment and is, therefore, religious, it fails to foster growth toward human development and wholeness. Rather, it is essentially escapist and disallows the attainment of wholeness.

On the other hand, one might argue that the secular approach to reality, as outlined in this study, is a fully authentic ontological and religious stance to the world because it provides an avenue toward human development and wholeness. Rather than encouraging escape from the complexity of life through the comfort of an otherworldly promise, the secularizing tendency in the nineteenth century allows one to locate the religiously significant within the present world. As a result, one who approaches the world in such a way may live within it more fully and gain a greater possibility for wholeness than someone who is oriented by otherworldliness. The person who approaches life religiously with a secular worldview may gain a greater appreciation for the natural world itself and for human worth and interpersonal relationships. While the religious *sacralist* can only appreciate the world and human beings through a dedication to otherworldly visions, the religious *secularist* appreciates the world for what it is and its people for who they are.

This secularized religious approach to reality hinges on the difference between sacred and secular space. This approach is religious because otherness is still a factor for secular people in search of meaning. The religious person who seeks otherness through transcendence has her counterpart in the secular world in the person for whom space itself is other. Meaning-giving otherness in the secular world presents itself through the physical and social environments—environments that exhibit both a benevolent and malevolent side as well as both a familiar and mysterious character. These familiar and strange worlds are no longer simply a means to otherness for the religious secularist. Rather, they constitute otherness itself.

With this analysis, I do not mean to suggest that the rise of secularity in religion dominated religious approaches to reality in the first part of this century. On the contrary, secular religious approaches to reality describe only a portion of the ways that Americans sought meaning at the beginning of the twentieth century. In fact, a renewal of a sacred approach to reality in the early part of this century, in the form of fundamentalism, constitutes a parallel, and in many ways reactionary, religious stance to secularized religion. What gave rise to a renewed interest in fundamentalism in the early twentieth century is the same thing that gave rise to secularity—the destruction and loss of familiar religious symbols and concepts. The fundamentalists attempted to make sense of their world by reaching back and recapturing lost ideals so that their world once again made sense in old, familiar terms, while the secularists attempted to redefine their world so that it made sense in light of new reality perceptions. The point of the comparison here is that both the rise of secularity and the growth of fundamentalism during this time period occurred in reaction to a common cultural and religious crisis; just as fundamentalism was not "a temporary social aberration, but . . . a genuine religious movement or tendency with deep roots and intelligible beliefs,"[14] so was the rise of secularity an equally valid religious approach to reality.

Nevertheless, this study involves more than a comparison of sacred and secular ways of approaching reality and of being religious. It also concerns itself with the transition from a sacred worldview to a secular one that occurred in the late nineteenth century and early twentieth century in America. This transition was one of reevaluation and restructuring of the dreams and myths upon which this country is built, and it resulted in a fundamental redefinition of the status of American space. The process of redefinition was one of affirmation, doubt, and reassessment, and it allowed Americans to move from a position of uncertainty to an experience of wholeness. Thus, the model of world construction (or reconstruction) is a model of dislocation and legitimation. It occurs in a situation where people are estranged or dislocated and find themselves unsettled by their environment. Through the process of doubt and reassessment, they once again find a world where they can rediscover their spatial centrality and ontological legitimacy. That this model of world construction offers meaning and wholeness makes it a religious model, and it assumes a religious process.

Furthermore, this process did not end in the 1920s, but rather continues in the 1980s and 1990s as Americans still struggle with the identity of their country as either a sacred or secular land. With this in mind, I extend this discussion of the religious redefinition of the American world to draw conclusions from this model for the study of "Religion and Culture" and "Religion and Literature" as disciplines. For through the tools of cultural analysis, one can understand better the dynamics that are involved as world construction and redefinition continue to take place.

4. The Religion and Culture Question: The Meaning-Granting Function of Religion and Literature

The process of world reconstruction—the process of affirmation, doubt, and reassessment, which I describe in this work, is a religious exercise in itself and is the key to my understanding of the relationship between religion and literature. This work begins with a functional definition of both religion and literature and concludes with the assertion that religion and literature both participate toward the same end—providing a world that grants human wholeness, meaning, and legitimacy. This study testifies to this process by means of a literary redefinition of a religious understanding of society and its exchange for a conflicting religious view of America.

However, there is a deeper relationship between the structure and function of religion and literature that highlights a fundamental wedding of the narrative form and religious expression as two functional and cultural participants involved in granting human meaning. This deeper relationship emerges from the ability of both religion and literature to move human beings from a situation of estrangement to a position of wholeness—from a world without a center to a world with ultimate meaning—from the horror of anonymity to the power of legitimacy.

This relationship evolves from the function of both literature and religion as necessary and important forms within a particular cultural setting. When dislocation occurs and when a group of people lose their sense of place in a world, the process of doubt and reassessment begins in order to relocate these "estrangers" to a meaningful position in another, redefined world. This process of redefinition occurs through cultural and public forms (for example, religion *and* literature), and it is reappropriated individually as people come into contact with such forms. Thus, religion and literature both play an important role within a cultural setting as cultural forms that encourage and participate in the process of world construction. They do so because religious and literary forms, within a particular culture, are parallel belief structures. The individuals who participate in these belief systems are able to evaluate and reevaluate their purpose and meaning as they interact with cultural forms that reinforce their need for legitimacy.

This functional understanding of religion and literature, which are forms that act in world construction, emanates from the cultural characteristics of both. One can say, for example, that narrative parallels the functional role of religion in providing status for disinherited and disenfranchised groups.[15] In the same way, narrative forms function to provide balance when equilibrium is lost and to allow meaningful change to take place; they are, therefore, meaning-laden.[16] Because religion and literature function in similar ways and because they represent parallel belief structures, the study of religion and literature should be a natural combination within a larger cultural studies program. Such a method for cultural studies finds support in theorists like Clifford Geertz and Peter Berger.

Clifford Geertz borrows an expression from Gilbert Ryle to describe his procedure for providing an interpretive analysis of culture; "thick description" represents Geertz's method of interpreting the social and cultural structures of humankind. Geertz posits a semiotic concept of culture and states that the analysis of culture is "an interpretive one in search of meaning." For Geertz, "man is . . . suspended in webs of significance he himself has spun."[17] These webs are the cultural structures that humankind has constructed. The duty of the ethnographer is to untangle the webs so that the animal, *Homo sapiens*, can struggle free and so that in this liberating struggle, meaning can be recognized and clarified.

Thus, for Geertz, any analysis of culture must be an hermeneutical one. This is especially relevant to the interpretive work of the critic or theologian, yet it is also true for the reader of a text or for the believer of a faith. They, too, seek to unravel the webs of significance so that they might glean truth and meaning from cultural structures.

Throughout his essay on "Thick Description," Geertz develops a type of hierarchy of cultural structures that allow for interpretation. Literature, art, and religion are highly symbolic cultural forms within this hierarchy. Furthermore, to study any cultural structure is to move toward an interpretive analysis of the social group behind that symbolic structure. For these cultural forms are nothing less than a particular group's attempt to place reality within a meaningful sphere of reference through the use of symbols. Thus, religion and literature "plunge into the midst" of the "existential dilemmas of life" and attempt to provide human beings with a world where meaning exists.[18] How cultural forms act to construct such a world is key to the understanding of the relationship of religion and literature. The process of this construction appears in the sociological work of Peter Berger and his concepts of externalization, objectivation, internalization, and legitimation.

According to Berger, human beings construct the worlds where they live, and in this distinctly human project, humanity produces society that in turn acts back and influences humankind. This social dialectic is inherent in human life collectively and individually and occurs in three stages—externalization, objectivation, and internalization. Thus, Berger writes,

> Externalization is the ongoing outpouring of human being into the world, both in the physical and the mental activity of men. Objectivation is the attainment by the products of this activity (again both physical and mental) of a reality that confronts its original producers as a facticity external to and other than themselves. Internalization is the reappropriation by men of this same reality, transforming it once again from structures of the objective world into structures of the subjective consciousness.[19]

This cultural process of externalization, objectivation, and internalization describes the religious process of worship and belief and the literary process of writing and reading. In both cases, the attainment of truth occurs when an objective truth is reappropriated individually (by the reader or believer) and redefined in a way that is valid for a changing world.[20] Yet, it also must be stressed that not only is the new belief a religious orientation, but the struggle or process of attaining that belief is religious as well. This religious process pervades religion, literature, and the process of the redefinition of American space that occurred in the latter nineteenth century and early twentieth century.

Thus, literature and religion are world building and involve the process of redefinition to create a world of meaning. Yet, how does this relate to the situation in the late nineteenth century when one world was shattered and its inhabitants became lost? In other words, how does this process of world building and reappropriation occur in relation to the phenomenon of dislocation? Dislocation seems to be the instigator of world construction and worldview redefinition, because it is with the loss of place that questions about one's world arise. Berger's principle of legitimation describes this movement from dislocation to relocation. Berger defines legitimation as

> socially objectivated "knowledge" that serves to explain and justify the social order. Put differently, legitimations are answers to any questions about the "why" of institutional arrangements.[21]

Thus, legitimation is a second order "objectivation of meaning" that justifies the first order objectivations such as religious experience, social reality, and narrative reading.[22] In other words, legitimations tend to make sense out of world reality. Legitimations justify and relocate the disinherited in their world by placing that world within an acceptable and familiar frame of reference. Legitimation is "reality-maintenance" and lends precarious reality perceptions some degree of validity.[23] In the case of the nineteenth century, the literature of the time period provided legitimations for a group of people who were disoriented in an unfamiliar world. This literature redefined that world so that once again its inhabitants could gain a sense of validity and purpose.

Berger's concept of legitimation parallels the function of narrative as A. J. Greimas understands it. For Greimas, narrative either supports a dominant worldview, or it provides the disinherited a means to overcome their intolerable situation.[24] This legitimating function of narrative operates to place a group within a meaningful world in a similar way that religion operates to elevate human beings to a position of worth. Both function religiously in the restorative process of doubt and redefinition. Both religion and literature operate within the totality of human experience, receiving impetus from that experience and acting upon experience, to provide wholeness and meaning for the participants in the human enterprise. Nevertheless, contrary to what might be assumed concerning this model, the functional role of religion and literature (religion and literature act to provide social, psychological, and spiritual wholeness) does not assume a conflictual model for world reconstruction. Social and economic models alone are not adequate for explaining religious changes in the late nineteenth and early twentieth centuries, because dislocation in America at this time extended beyond class lines and struggles.

5. Summary

This study, which began with the bifurcated American dream of physical and social sacred opportunity, has proceeded from Cather's and Dreiser's rejection of and redefinition of this bipolar dream, through the emergence of a new secular world around the turn of the century, to theoretical conclusions on the religiosity of secularity and on the mutual roles of religion and literature in world-definition. With the end of this development, this work has reached its conclusion, and its results can be summarized. The results are positive in several respects. First, an examination of the American dream in its physical and social manifestations is helpful in explicating many of the confusions concerning disillusionment and disappointment over the American way. Second, Dreiser and Cather, in a way that moves beyond their stereotyping as a naturalist and a regionalist, should be placed squarely within the changing scene of *fin de siècle* America as they are here. Third, their work helps to clarify some issues concerning the role of religion and literature in cultural change. Finally, I hope that I have shown that the process of cultural redefinition must be constant if human beings are to live meaningfully within their world. Thus, the present tensions that exist between conflicting worldviews can be healthy if interplay occurs in such a way that any one view does not exert sole and final authority. Rather, conflicting worldviews must constantly question and reevaluate one another as the quest for meaning continues within either a religious or a literary context. For it is also in that quest itself, and not only in its results, that one can find, study, and evaluate the religious qualities of cultural change.

Notes

Chapter 1. "America" as Paradise Lost

1. John Winthrop, "A Modell of Christian Charity," *Winthrop Papers, 1623–1630,* vol. 2 (Boston: Massachusetts Historical Society, 1931), as reproduced in H. Shelton Smith, Robert T. Handy, and Lefferts A. Loetscher, *American Christianity: An Historical Interpretation with Representative Documents,* vol. 1 (New York: Charles Scribner's Sons, 1960), p. 102.

2. Sacvan Bercovitch, *The American Jeremiad* (Madison: University of Wisconsin Press, 1978), "Preface" and p. 94. The idea of America's myth of election and opportunity receives development from scores of writers in American studies. For the development of these ideas, see David Noble, *The Eternal Adam and the New World Garden: The Central Myth in the American Novel Since 1830* (New York: Braziller, 1968), pp. ix–xi; Howard Mumford Jones, *The Frontier in American Fiction: Four Lectures on the Relation of Landscape to Literature* (Jerusalem: The Magness Press, 1956), pp. 9, 16; and Alfred Kazin, *An American Procession: The Major American Writers from 1830–1930—The Crucial Century* (New York: Vintage Books, Random House, 1985), pp. 44, 57–58.

3. For the best treatment of this aspect of the Puritan mission in the New World, see Perry Miller, *Errand Into the Wilderness* (Cambridge: Harvard University Press, 1956). See also Peter N. Carroll, *Puritanism and the Wilderness: The Intellectual Significance of the New England Frontier, 1629–1700* (New York: Columbia University Press, 1969).

4. Bercovitch, *American Jeremiad,* pp. 47ff., 135–36, 121.

5. Ibid., pp. 178–79.

6. Ibid., "Epilogue."

7. Catherine L. Albanese, *America: Religions and Religion* (Belmont, Calif.: Wadsworth Publishing Company, 1981), p. 332.

8. Herman Melville, *Moby Dick or The White Whale* (New York: New American Library, 1961, chap. 1, p. 23; Giles Gunn, *The Interpretation of Otherness: Literature, Religion, and the American Imagination* (New York: Oxford University Press, 1979), p. 171; Emerson, "The Poet," p. 19, and "The American Scholar," p. 75, both in R. E. Spiller, ed., *Selected Essays, Lectures, and Poems of Ralph Waldo Emerson* (New York: Simon and Schuster, 1965); and Gunn, *The Interpretation of Otherness,* p. 171.

9. Melville, *Moby Dick,* chap. 2, p. 26.

10. Richard Poirier, *A World Elsewhere: The Place of Style in American Literature* (London: Oxford University Press, 1966), pp. 42, 7.

11. Ibid., p. 42.

12. Charles Child Walcutt, "Theodore Dreiser and the Divided Stream," in Alfred Kazin and Charles Shapiro, eds., *The Stature of Theodore Dreiser* (Bloomington: Indiana University Press, 1955), p. 246.

13. See R. W. B. Lewis, "Hold on Hard to the Huckleberry Bushes," in Lewis, *Trials of the Word: Essays in American Literature and the Humanistic Tradition* (New Haven: Yale University Press, 1965), pp. 108ff.; Tony Tanner, *The Reign of Wonder: Naivety and Reality in American Literature* (Cambridge: The University Press, 1965), pp. 29, 36ff.; and Emerson, "Nature," in Spiller, *Selected Essays*, p. 181.

14. Emerson, "Nature," in Spiller, *Selected Essays*, p. 181.

15. This benevolent picture of nature is prevalent in Thoreau's writing, also. Thoreau approaches nature as the key to a meaningful existence in this world. For one to experience fulfillment, one must participate in "wildness" and seek communion with the natural forces of the animal and vegetable world. In *Walden*, this participation in wildness comes in the form of overcoming the brute self in order to enjoy a peaceful union with the natural realm. The brute self— the animal self—seeks to dominate nature and stands in the way of any meaningful co-existence with the natural. Thus, by transcending the brute self, one can commune with a sacred natural world and come to a greater spiritual awareness of humanity and of humanity's place in the cosmos. See also Henry David Thoreau, "Wild Apples," in Henry Seidel Canby, ed., *The Works of Thoreau* (Boston: Houghton Mifflin Co., 1937), p. 718.

16. Tanner, *The Reign of Wonder*, pp. 5, 7.

17. Emerson, "The Poet," in Spiller, *Selected Essays*, p. 18.

18. J. Hillis Miller, *Poets of Reality: Six Twentieth Century Writers* (New York: Atheneum, 1974), pp. 1–2. See also Gunn, *The Interpretation of Otherness*, p. 188, and Tanner, *The Reign of Wonder*, p. 30.

19. See William R. Hutchison, *The Modernist Impulse in American Protestantism* (Oxford: Oxford University Press, 1976). Hutchison traces what he calls the "modernist impulse" through nineteenth-century liberalism.

20. George Ripley to Ralph Waldo Emerson, Emerson Papers, Houghton, about October 1840, as quoted in Anne C. Rose, *Transcendentalism as a Social Movement, 1830–1850* (New Haven: Yale University Press, 1981), p.93.

21. Rose, *Transcendentalism as a Social Movement*, p. 93.

22. Mark Holloway, *Heavens on Earth: Utopian Communities in America: 1680–1880* (London: Tunstile Press, 1951), pp. 128–29; and Rose, *Transcendentalism as a Social Movement*, pp. 134–35.

23. Holloway, *Heavens on Earth*, p. 130.

24. Elizabeth Peabody, "A Glimpse of Christ's Idea of Society," *Dial* 2 (October 1841): 222, as quoted by Rose, *Transcendentalism as a Social Movement*, p. 93.

25. Poirier, *A World Elsewhere*.

26. Emerson, "The Poet," in Spiller, *Selected Essays*, p. 18.

27. Emerson, "Nature, Introduction," in Spiller, *Selected Essays*, p. 179; and "Nature," in Spiller, *Selected Essays*, pp. 181–82.

28. Walt Whitman, "Song of Myself," in John Kouwenhoven, ed., *Leaves of Grass and Selected Prose* (New York: The Modern Library, Random House, 1950), 31, p. 49, and (48, pp. 72–73.

29. These images of sacred physical and social space are represented respectively by the Turner thesis of western expansion and by the emphasis placed on development of urban space at the World's Columbian Exposition of 1893 in Chicago. My point is that during the last half of the nineteenth century, changing conceptions of natural and social space were prevalent in and important to cultural transitions in America.

30. Gunn, *The Interpretation of Otherness*, pp. 120ff. and 174–75.

31. M. H. Abrams, *Natural Supernaturalism* (New York: W. W. Norton and Company, 1971), p. 68.

32. Ibid., pp. 13ff.

33. Perry Miller, ed., *American Thought: Civil War to World War I* (New York: Rinehart and Company, 1954), p. ix.

34. The allusion to playing the game by Darwin's rules comes from a lecture by Grant Wacker in "Introduction to the History of Religion in America," 30 October 1984.

35. Granville Hicks, "Theodore Dreiser," in *The American Mercury* 62 (June 1946): 752.

36. See Ferenc Morton Szasz, *The Divided Mind of Protestant America, 1880–1930* (Tuscaloosa: The University of Alabama Press, 1982), and William R. Hutchison, *The Modernist Impulse in American Protestantism* (Oxford: Oxford University Press, 1976).

37. Henry Nash Smith, *Virgin Land: The American West as Symbol and Myth* (Cambridge: Harvard University Press, 1950), pp. 123, 133, 155.

38. Ibid., pp. 153, 162, 187.

39. Leo Marx, *Machine in the Garden* (New York: Oxford University Press, 1964), p. 58.

40. Ibid., pp. 105, 76, 131.

41. Ibid.

42. Smith, *Virgin Land*, pp. 235–36.

43. Ibid., p. 89.

44. Perry Miller, ed., *American Thought*, "Introduction."

45. Gunn, *Interpretation of Otherness*, pp. 174–75.

46. Miller, *American Thought*, pp. xvii, xiv.

47. See John D. Hicks, *The Populist Revolt* (Lincoln: The University of Nebraska Press, 1961).

48. See Szasz, *The Divided Mind*, and Hutchison, *The Modernist Impulse in American Protestantism*.

49. The realistic literary movement in America is particularly suited to usher in this redefinition of American space. Not only does realism emphasize objectivity and telling the truth, but this objectivity emerges as a methodology for describing Darwinian and Spencerian determinism. Thus, as a literary philosophy, realism is uniquely armed to present the world in unsettling deterministic categories. Jane Benardete extends this understanding of realism to her definition of naturalism. Naturalism also seeks to locate the truth, but naturalistic emphasis shifts to survival in the objective world while it neglects the moral response to truth. While naturalistic literature does emphasize survival, it does not necessarily reject the moral response to the world. I hope to demonstrate this with the chapter on Theodore Dreiser. Nevertheless, realism and naturalism play an active role in the redefinition of American space as methodologies as well as philosophies. Realistic literature is not simply a response to social forces as Alfred Kazin seems to suggest in *On Native Grounds*. See Richard Ellman and Charles Feidelson, Jr., *The Modern Tradition: Backgrounds of Modern Literature* (New York: Oxford University Press, 1965), pp. 229ff.; Jane Benardete, *American Realism* (New York: G. P. Putman's Sons, 1972), pp. 23ff.; and Alfred Kazin, *On Native Grounds: An Interpretation of Modern American Prose Literature* (New York: Harcourt, Brace and Company, 1942).

50. Lee T. Lemon, "The Hostile Universe: A Developing Pattern in Nineteenth-Century Fiction," in George Goodin, ed., *The English Novel in the*

Nineteenth Century: Essays on the Literary Mediation of Human Values (Chicago: University of Illinois Press, 1972), p. 12. See also pp. 1–2, 6–7, 11–12.

51. For the role of the visionary character as I use it here see Wesley A. Kort, *Moral Fiber: Characters and Belief in American Fiction* (Philadelphia: Fortress Press, 1982), pp. 13, 92, 135ff. The visionary character is one who is capable of envisioning "imagined, projected, or intuited forms of transcendent coherence and wholeness" in the face of "incompleteness or confusion of experience." Such characters are "oriented to the transcendent" especially in the confrontation of otherness in the world. It is the "whole person" born of wisdom who is capable of remaining open to possibility and world-altering views in face of ontologically threatening circumstances. See Kort, *Moral Fiber,* pp. 13, 92, 135ff.

52. Timothy S. Bauer-Yocum, "In Search of a Myth for Modern America: Spiritual and Cultural Renewal in Walt Whitman and Henry Adams" (Ph. D. diss., Duke University, 1983), pp. 8ff., 19. See also John F. Wilson, *Public Religion in American Culture* (Philadelphia: Temple University Press, 1979).

53. See Giles Gunn, *New World Metaphysics.* See also Bauer-Yocum, "In Search of a Myth," pp. 8ff.

54. I began to seek continuities between Cather and Dreiser in response to my reading of Kenny Williams. She seems to suggest some type of unity underneath their widely differing writing styles in Kenny Williams, *In The City of Men: Another Story of Chicago* (Nashville, Tenn.: Townsend Press, 1974), pp. 382–83.

55. This quotation comes from Wesley A. Kort during conversations with him concerning this book.

Chapter 2. Living on the Edge of a World

1. Cather scholarship is dominated by the critical biography. There are numerous studies that draw inferences between Cather's life and the effect her experiences play upon the creation of her fiction. Since my primary objective is not critical biography, I shall mention the best of these studies here for further reference. The best full length biographies of Willa Cather are Mildred R. Bennett, *The World of Willa Cather* (New York: Dodd, Mead, and Company, 1951), and E. K. Brown, *Willa Cather: A Critical Biography* (New York: Alfred A. Knopf, 1953). An excellent summary of Cather's life and works appears in Henry James Forman, "Willa Cather: A Voice from the Prairie," *Southwest Review* 47 (Summer 1962): 248–58. See also David Stouck, *Willa Cather's Imagination* (Lincoln: University of Nebraska Press, 1975).

2. Brown, *Willa Cather,* pp. 48, v–vi.

3. Russell Blankenship, *American Literature As An Expression of the National Mind* (New York: Henry Holt and Company, 1931), p. 677. See also David Daiches, *Willa Cather: A Critical Introduction* (New York: Cornell University Press, 1951), p. 18.

4. John H. Randall, III, "Willa Cather and the Pastoral Tradition," in John J. Murphy, ed., *Five Essays on Willa Cather: The Merrimack Symposium* (North Andover, Mass.: Merrimack College, 1974).

5. For this understanding of setting or "atmosphere," see Wesley A. Kort, *Narrative Elements and Religious Meaning* (Philadelphia: Fortress Press, 1975), pp. 20ff. I have chosen to deal with setting, because setting seems to dominate Ca-

ther's prairie novels. Nevertheless, other critics tend to isolate one of the other four literary elements as the dominant characteristic of Cather's fiction. For example, John H. Randall and a myriad of critics isolate plot and narrative time as the predominant element in Cather's fiction. See John H. Randall, *The Landscape and the Looking Glass: Willa Cather's Search for Value* (Boston: Houghton Mifflin Company), 1960. Edward A. and Lillian D. Bloom reduce the importance of both setting and plot and tend to emphasize tone in Cather's work. See Edward A. and Lillian D. Bloom, "Willa Cather's Novel's of the Frontier: A Study in Thematic Symbolism" in *American Literature* 21 (March 1949): 71–93. Finally, Lionel Trilling focuses upon the character of the pioneer in the face of failure as the dominant element in Cather's novels. See Lionel Trilling, "Willa Cather" in James Schroeter, *Willa Cather and Her Critics* (Ithaca: Cornell University Press, 1967), pp. 148–55.

6. See Sister Lucy Schneider, C.S.J., "Willa Cather's Early Stories in the Light of Her 'Land Philosophy'," *The Midwest Quarterly* 9 (October 1967): 75, 77; and Sister Lucy Schneider, C.S.J., "Artistry and Instinct: Willa Cather's 'Land Philosophy'," *College Language Association Journal* 16 (June 1973): 488.

7. Schneider, "Artistry and Instinct," pp. 485–87.

8. See Theodore S. Adams, "Willa Cather's *My Mortal Enemy:* The Concise Presentation of Scene, Character, and Theme," *Colby Library Quarterly* 10 (September 1973): 146. See also Daiches, *Willa Cather: A Critical Introduction.* For the theme of the land as a symbol of opportunity and transcendence, see Frederick Tabor Cooper, "Review" of *O Pionners!*, in John J. Murphy, ed., *Critical Essays on Willa Cather* (Boston: G. K. Hall & Co., 1984), p. 17; Daiches, *Willa Cather: A Critical Introduction*, p. 23; Granville Hicks, "The Case Against Willa Cather," in Schroeter, *Willa Cather and Her Critics*, p. 139ff.; Alfred Kazin, "Willa Cather," in Schroeter, *Willa Cather and Her Critics*, p. 164; Edward A. and Lillian D. Bloom, *Willa Cather's Gift of Sympathy* (Carbondale: Southern Illinois University Press, 1962), pp. 14–15, 16, 22; and Paul C. Wermuth, "Willa Cather's Virginia Novel," *Virginia Calvalcade* 7 (Spring 1958): 4–7.

9. See also Daiches, *Willa Cather: A Critical Introduction;* Bloom, *Willa Cather's Gift of Sympathy;* John J. Murphy, "Cooper, Cather, and the Downward Path to Progress," *Prairie Schooner* 55 (Spring/Summer 1981): 168–84; and J. M. Ferguson, Jr., "'Vague Outlines': Willa Cather's Enchanted Bluffs" *Western Review* 7 (Spring 1970): 61–64.

10. Sister Lucy Schneider, C.S.J., "*O Pioneers!* in the Light of Willa Cather's 'Land Philosophy'," *Colby Library Quarterly* 8 (June 1968): 56–57; Schneider, "Cather's 'Land Philosophy' in *Death Comes for the Archbishop*," *Renascence* 22 (Winter 1970): 78–79; and Schneider, "Artistry and Instinct," pp. 485–87.

11. For such a view, see Hicks, "The Case Against Willa Cather."

12. "Prairie Spring" appears as a preface to Willa Cather, *O Pioneers!* (Willa Sibert Cather, 1913 and 1914). Reprinted by permission of Houghton Mifflin Company.

13. See Hicks, "The Case Against Willa Cather," pp. 139ff. for the development of these themes.

14. For Cather's reference to homesickness, see "Prairie Dawn," in Ernest Boyd, ed., *Modern American Writers*, (New York: R. M. McBride and Company, 1930), vol. 8: *Willa Cather*, Rene Rapin, p. 16. For a view of nature as forbidding, see James E. Miller, Jr., "The Nebraska Encounter: Willa Cather and Wright Morris," *Prairie Schooner* 41 (Summer 1967): 167; Adams, "Willa Cather's *My Mortal Enemy;* and Daiches, *Willa Cather: A Critical Introduction.* For the theme of

nature as beneficent in Cather's fiction, see Kazin, "Willa Cather," and Bloom, *Willa Cather's Gift of Sympathy.*

15. Rudolf Otto discusses the "awefulness" and the mysteriousness of the "holy." The idea of the holy, or the other, must include this element of mystery, power, and harshness if it is to be considered that which is truly other. See Rudolf Otto, *The Idea of the Holy: An Inquiry into the Non-Rational Factor in the Idea of the Divine and its Relation to the Rational*, translated by John W. Harvey (London: Oxford University Press, 1928), pp. 12ff. See also G. van der Leeuw, *Religion in Essence and Manifestation: A Study in Phenomenology*, translated by J. E. Turner (London: George Allen and Unwin, 1938), especially part 1.

16. Wermuth, "Willa Cather's Virginia Novel," p. 6–7. For more development of the hostility theme, see Randall, *The Landscape and the Looking Glass*, p. 65. James E. Miller further asserts that the seasons add an element of hostility to the already rough environment. The prairie in winter "seems indifferent to man, hostile to life." See James E. Miller, Jr., "The Nebraska Encounter," p. 167. See also Geismar, "Willa Cather: Lady in the Wilderness," p. 178.

17. Willa Cather, *O Pioneers!* (Boston: Houghton Mifflin Company, 1913), pp. 21–22.

18. Willa Cather, *My Ántonia* (Boston: Houghton Mifflin Company, 1918), p.159. The abandoned "plough" image is one of the most famous and the most quoted of the passages from *My Ántonia.* Critics interpret its symbolic significance in a variety of ways ranging from a symbol of defeat and abandonment to a symbol of the heroic struggle that the pioneer exhibited. The predominant force of the symbol seems to be one of abandonment that highlights the futility of the pioneers' heroism in the face of an indifferent environment.

19. Randall, *The Landscape and the Looking Glass*, p. 65.

20. For determinism in Cather's work, see Willa Cather, "Paul's Case" in *Youth and the Bright Medusa* (New York: Vintage Books, Random House, 1975), pp. 201–2. Also, determinism and the helplessness of human beings in the face of nature occur more often in Cather's early stories and prairie novels. See Marilyn Arnold, *Willa Cather's Short Fiction* (Athens: Ohio University Press, 1984), p. 2, and Randall, *The Landscape and the Looking Glass*, p. 66.

21. Robert Edson Lee, *From West to East: Studies in the Literature of the American West* (Urbana: University of Illinois Press, 1966), pp. 114–15.

22. Eudora Welty, "The House of Cather" in the Alderman Library, *Miracles of Perception: The Art of Willa Cather* (Charlottesville: University of Virginia, 1980), pp. 22, 21. See also Randall, *The Landscape and the Looking Glass*, p. 84. Randall asserts that nature governs emotions. For example, in *O Pioneers!*, the passion of Marie and Emil, and Frank's rage, are emotions springing from the internal nature of the characters.

23. Arnold, *Willa Cather's Short Fiction*, p. 88. Imprisonment takes on a quite literal meaning in *Sapphira and the Slave Girl.* See Dorothy Canfield Fisher, "Review of *Sapphira and the Slave Girl*," in John J. Murphy, *Critical Essays on Willa Cather* (Boston: G. K. Hall and Company, 1984), p. 285.

24. Cather, *O Pioneers!*, pp. 122–24. See also Sister Peter Damian Charles, O.P., "Love and Death in Willa Cather's *O Pioneers!*," *CLA Journal* 9 (December 1965): 144. Willa Cather herself experienced this type of emotional isolation and the need to escape while she lived in Red Cloud, Nebraska. See Dorothy Van Ghent, *Willa Cather* (Minneapolis: University of Minnesota Press, 1964), p. 6. Other examples in Cather's fiction of this emotional isolation occur in *My Ántonia, The Professor's House*, "A Wagner Matinee," and "A Death in the Desert."

See Cather, *The Professor's House* (London: Hamish Hamilton, 1961), pp. 30ff.; Cather, "A Wagner Matinee," in *Youth and the Bright Medusa*, pp. 222, 226; Cather, "A Death in the Desert," in *Youth and the Bright Medusa;* Rapin, *Willa Cather*, p. 50; and Wallace Stegner, "Willa Cather, *My Ántonia*," in Wallace Stegner, ed., *The American Novel: From James Fenimore Cooper to William Faulkner* (New York: Basic Books, Inc., 1965), p. 148.

25. Daiches, *Willa Cather: A Critical Introduction*, pp. 27ff.

26. See Mencken, "Review" of *One of Ours*, in Schroeter, *Willa Cather and Her Critics*, p. 11. For a further discussion of the stifling effects of Claude's environment, see Daiches, *Willa Cather: A Critical Introduction*, pp. 62ff.; and Murphy, "Willa Cather: The Widening Gyre," pp. 61–62.

27. Cather, *My Ántonia*, p. 25.

28. Wilson, "Two Novels of Willa Cather," pp. 28–29.

29. Marginality in Cather's work is best identified in the prevalent theme of cultural complexity. Although Cather usually appears to be a regional writer, this conception is much too narrow for her. As Elizabeh Monroe writes, Cather writes of "a new settlement of the frontier by Swedes, Norwegians, Poles, Slavs, Bohemians, and the French, the contrast between the civilizations involved in this settlement, the sweep of American religious history, and the triumph of great personalities over the hardships of American life." See Elizabeth Monroe, *The Novel and Society* (Chapel Hill: University of North Carolina Press, 1941), quoted in Edward Wagenknecht, *Cavalcade of the American Novel: From the Birth of the Nation to the Middle of the Twentieth Century* (New York: Holt, Rinehart and Winston, 1952), p. 319. For a further discussion on the treatment of immigrants in Cather's work, see Howard Mumford Jones, *The Frontier in American Fiction: Four Lectures on the Relation of Landscape to Literature* (Jerusalem: The Magness Press, 1956), pp. 78ff. The problem of cultural complexity usually occurs as a problem of new and old institutions clashing. "Grounded deeply in the American soil, the novels of Willa Cather nevertheless are attached also by visible threads to roots in the Old World." See Brown, *Willa Cather: A Critical Biography*, p. 99, and Cooper, "Review" of *O Pioneers!*, pp. 16–17. Cultural complexity in Cather's work also occurs within the American boundaries. For example, in "A Wagner Matinee," the cultural "lack" of the West contrasts to the cultural forms of Boston. Furthermore, in "Old Mrs. Harris," the cultural forms of European civilization clash on the frontier with traditional Southern feudalism and the new Western democracy. See Cather, "A Wagner Matinee," and Cather, "Old Mrs. Harris," in Cather, *Obscure Destinies* (New York: Vintage Books, Random House, 1974).

30. Willa Cather, *A Lost Lady* (New York: Vintage Books, Random House, 1972), p. 125.

31. Willa Cather, *Death Comes for the Archbishop* (New York: Vintage Books, Random House, 1971), p. 274.

32. See Wesley Kort, *Narrative Elements*, pp. 20–39 for a development of this understanding of "atmosphere."

33. See Edward A. and Lillian D. Bloom, *Willa Cather's Gift to Sympathy*, pp. 77, 78, and 83ff., and Bloom, "Willa Cather's Novels of the Frontier," p. 22. See also Cooper, "Review" of *O Pioneers!*, p. 112.

34. See Daiches, *Willa Cather: A Critical Introduction*, p. 79. Daiches sees Captain Forrester as symbolic of the noble frontier hero. See also Stouk, *Willa Cather's Imagination*, p. 2. Stouk cites heroism of the pioneers as one of the themes that makes Cather's work so complex.

35. See Trilling, "Willa Cather," p. 149. See also Daiches, *Willa Cather: A Critical Introduction,* p. 86.

36. See Geismar, "Willa Cather: Lady in the Wilderness," p. 177; and Brown, *Willa Cather: A Critical Biography,* p. 331.

37. See Patrick J. Sullivan, "Willa Cather's Southwest" in *Western American Literature* 7 (Spring 1972): 25–37. Sullivan maintains that the settled western frontier is one step removed from the west as sacred ground and that the humanizing of the frontier is the first step toward the decline of the west.

38. For the liberation quote, see Bloom, *Willa Cather's Gift of Sympathy,* p. 19. For the theme and characteristics of the west as sacred land, see Maynard Fox, "Proponents of Order: Tom Outland and Bishop Latour" in *Western American Literature* 4 (Summer 1969): 108; and Randall, *The Landscape and the Looking Glass,* p. 75.

39. John J. Murphy, "Cooper, Cather, and the Downward Path to Progress" in *Prairie Schooner* 55 (Spring/Summer 1981): 173; and Bloom, *Willa Cather's Gift of Sympathy,* 21.

40. Bernard Baum, "Willa Cather's Waste Land" in *The South Atlantic Quarterly* 48 (October 1949): 590.

41. See Patricia Lee Yongue, "*A Lost Lady:* The End of the First Cycle" in *Western American Literature* 7 (Spring 1972): 6–9. See also Daiches, *Willa Cather: A Critical Introduction,* p. 78; and Murphy, "Willa Cather: The Widening Gyre," p. 66.

42. For the tension between the land and civilization in *My Ántonia,* see Bloom, *Willa Cather's Gift of Sympathy,* pp. 9–10; Jones, *The Frontier in American Fiction,* p. 83; and Stegner, "Willa Cather, *My Ántonia,*" pp. 148ff.

43. Cather, "Neighbour Rosicky," (New York: Vintage Books, Random House, 1974. Originally published by Alfred A. Knopf, Inc., 1932), pp. 59–60.

44. Cather, *The Professor's House,* pp. 68ff. See also Willa Cather, *Alexander's Bridge* (Boston: Houghton Mifflin, 1912); and Geismar, "Willa Cather: Lady in the Wilderness," p. 186. For a discussion of the rise of the "cult of machinery" in *One of Ours,* see Brown, *Willa Cather: A Critical Biography,* pp. 219ff.

45. Murphy, "Cooper, Cather, and the Downward Path to Progress," pp. 168, 179 and Bloom, *Willa Cather's Gift of Sympathy,* p. 23.

46. Murphy, "Cooper, Cather, and the Downward Path to Progress," p. 181. Murphy quotes from *One of Ours.* See Willa Cather, *One of Ours* (New York: Vintage Books, Random House, 1971), p. 88.

47. See Murphy, "Cooper, Cather, and the Downward Path to Progress," pp. 174–75 and 176–77.

48. Jones, *The Frontier in American Fiction,* p. 89.

49. Cather, *A Lost Lady,* p. 118. See also Murphy, "Cooper, Cather, and the Downward Path to Progress," pp. 180–81.

50. Trilling, "Willa Cather," p. 151.

51. Van Ghent, *Willa Cather,* p. 6.

52. Bloom, "Willa Cather's Novels of the Frontier," p. 89.

53. Cather, *Death Comes For the Archbishop,* p. 295.

54. See Judith Fryer, "Cather's Felicitous Space," in *Prairie Schooner* (Spring/Summer 1981): 196; Fox, "Proponents of Order: Tom Outland and Bishop Latour," pp. 111–12; and Schneider, "Cather's 'Land-Philosophy' in *Death Comes For the Archbishop,*" p. 81 for descriptions of the Indian's sacred understanding of and approach to the land.

55. Cather, *Death Comes For the Archbishop,* p. 295.

56. Schneider, "Cather's 'Land-Philosophy' in *Death Comes For the Archbishop*," p. 82.

57. Sullivan, "Willa Cather's Southwest," p. 34.

58. See Brown, *Willa Cather: A Critical Biography*, pp. 176–77. The wild land appears superior in Cather's *Shadows on the Rock* as well. See Brown, *Willa Cather: A Critical Biography*, p. 285.

59. Schneider, "*O Pioneers!* in the Light of Willa Cather's 'Land Philosophy'," pp. 59–60.

60. Cather, *O Pioneers!*, p. 271.

61. Cather, *My Ántonia*, p. 28.

62. See Cather, *My Ántonia* and Daiches, *Willa Cather: A Critical Introduction*, pp. 47, 56. The theme of the land providing freedom appears elsewhere in Cather's fiction. The following quote appears in "Neighbour Rosicky." "To be a landless man was to be a wage-earner, a slave, all your life; to have nothing, to be nothing." See Willa Cather, "Neighbour Rosicky," in *Obscure Destinies*, p. 40.

63. Phyllis C. Robinson, *Willa: The Life of Willa Cather* (Garden City, N.Y.: Doubleday and Company, 1983), 175.

64. Fryer, "Cather's Felicitous Space," pp. 185–86.

65. Sullivan, "Willa Cather's Southwest," p. 29.

66. The "vague mystic experience" quote is from Bloom, "Willa Cather's Novels of the Frontier: A Study in Thematic Symbolism," p. 90, fn. 44. The second quote is from Fox, "Proponents of Order: Tom Outland and Bishop Latour," p. 110.

67. See, for example, Marilyn Arnold, *Willa Cather's Short Fiction*.

68. See Sullivan, "Willa Cather's Southwest," p. 28; Daiches, *Willa Cather: A Critical Introduction*, pp. 38ff.; and Brown, *Willa Cather: A Critical Biography*, pp. xii, xiii.

69. J. M. Ferguson, Jr., "'Vague Outlines': Willa Cather's Enchanted Bluffs," in *Western Review* 7 (Spring 1970): 62.

70. Ferguson, "'Vague Outlines'," p. 63. For the development of the parallel themes and narratives in *The Professor's House*, see Kazin, "Willa Cather," p. 169; and Van Ghent, *Willa Cather*, p. 29.

71. Cather, *The Professor's House*, p. 251, and Arnold, *Willa Cather's Short Fiction*, p. 83.

72. Cather, *The Professor's House*, p. 221. See also Sullivan, "Willa Cather's Southwest," p. 30.

73. For "Mother Eve," see Cather, *The Professor's House*, p. 214. For a description of the Cliff City as Garden of Eden paradise, see *The Professor's House*, pp. 201–2. For a description of the Blue Mesa as sacred land, see *The Professor's House*, pp. 186ff. and p. 194. The following quote is from p. 194 and describes Tom's first sensation of the sacred significance of the land on the mesa.

To people off alone, as we were, there is something stirring about finding evidences of human labour and care in the soil of an empty country. It comes to you as a sort of message, makes you feel differently about the ground you walk over every day.

For Tom, and in Cather's fiction in general, a sense of the sacrality of natural space involves a deep respect and reverence for the land as it is. This type of reverence is lacking in the pioneers that tame and desecrate the land for material gain.

74. Cather, *The Professor's House,* p. 270.

75. Murphy, "Cooper, Cather, and the Downward Path to Progress," p. 171.

76. Ernest Earnest, "The American Ariel," in *The South Atlantic Quarterly* 65 (Spring 1966): 200.

77. Murphy, "Cooper, Cather, and the Downward Path to Progress," p. 170.

78. Baum, "Willa Cather's Waste Land," p. 596.

79. See Schneider, "*O Pioneers!* in the Light of Willa Cather's 'Land-Philosophy'," p. 67.

80. Alexandra's extension of passionate feelings to the land is a highly recognized theme in *O Pioneers!* For the development of this theme, see Murphy, "A Comprehensive View of Cather's *O Pioneers!,*" p. 121, Murphy, "Willa Cather: The Widening Gyre," pp. 53–54; and Randall, *The Landscape and the Looking Glass,* pp. 67, 73. Randall discusses the personification of the land to account for the fact that the land arouses human feelings as if the land itself were human. Thus, Alexandra gives herself to the land instead of giving herself to others in terms of meaningful relationships. The land is a substitute for the missing erotic element between Alexandra and Carl.

81. Cather, *O Pioneers!,* pp. 205–6.

82. Ibid.

83. Rapin, *Willa Cather,* p. 22. See also Charles, "Love and Death in Willa Cather's *O Pioneers!,*" p. 140.

84. Cather, *O Pioneers!,* pp. 10ff. and Murphy, "A Comprehensive View of Cather's *O Pionners!,*" p. 114.

85. Cather, *O Pioneers!,* p. 271.

86. For an examination of *The Song of the Lark* using the Ariel model, see Earnest, "The American Ariel," pp. 193–95ff. For discussions of other failed relationships within the Cather corpus, see Lavon Mattes Jobes, "Willa Cather's Last Novel," in *The University Review* 34 (October 1967): pp. 78ff.; Murphy, "Willa Cather: The Widening Gyre;" and Trilling, "Willa Cather," p. 155.

87. Trilling, "Willa Cather," p. 154. For the isolation theme, see also Murhpy, "Willa Cather: The Widening Gyre," p. 59.

88. Arnold, *Willa Cather's Short Fiction,* p. 5.

89. See Arnold, *Willa Cather's Short Fiction* for a discussion of the isolation theme in Cather's early short work. See also Lee, *From West to East,* p. 119.

90. See Richard Giannone, *Music in Willa Cather's Fiction* (Lincoln: University of Nebraska Press, 1968), p. 207. For the last quote, see Arnold, *Willa Cather's Short Fiction,* p. 134.

91. See Geismar, "Willa Cather: Lady in the Wilderness," pp. 183–87; Trilling, "Willa Cather," p. 56, 51–52; Brown, *Willa Cather: A Critical Biography,* p. 224; and Daiches, *Willa Cather: A Critical Introduction,* pp. 72–74ff.

92. Willa Cather, "The Diamond Mine," in *Youth and the Bright Medusa* (New York: Vintage Books, Random House, 1975), p. 116.

93. Arnold, *Willa Cather's Short Fiction,* p. 10.

94. Cather, "Neighbour Rosicky," pp. 69–71.

95. Cather, *O Pioneers!,* pp. 303, 309.

96. See Murphy, "A Comprehensive View of Cather's *O Pioneers!,*" pp. 126–27.

97. Wesley A. Kort, *Moral Fiber: Character and Belief in Recent American Fiction* (Philadelphia: Fortress Press, 1982), pp. 33–44.

98. Ibid., p. 36.

99. Ibid., p. 38.

Chapter 3. The Exorcism of the Supernatural

1. Herbert J. Muller, *Modern Fiction: A Study of Values.* (New York: Funk and Wagnalls Co., 1937), p. 207, and Alfred Kazin, *An American Procession: The Major American Writers from 1830–1930—The Crucial Century.* (New York: Vintage Books, Random House, 1984), p. 336.

2. Alfred Kazin, "Introduction," in *The Stature of Theodore Dreiser,* eds. Alfred Kazin and Charles Shapiro (Bloomington: Indiana University Press, 1955), p. 5. Kazin offers a discussion on the unsettling effect that this new movement represented in American life.

3. Mircea Eliade, *The Sacred and the Profane: The Nature of Religion.* trans. Willard R. Trask (New York: Harcourt Brace Jovanovich, 1959), pp. 11, 22ff.

4. Ibid., 14, 23ff.

5. Kazin, "Introduction," p. 11.

6. David W. Noble. *The Eternal Adam and The New World Garden: The Central Myth in the American Novel Since 1830* (New York: Braziller, 1968), p. 124.

7. Randall Stewart, "Dreiser and the Naturalist Heresy," *Virginia Quarterly Review* 34 (Winter 1958): 102, 115. Stewart's criticism is damaged by his dogmatic adherence to the doctrine of original sin. He tends to judge all literature by this standard. However, his point concerning Dreiser's relationship to romantic literature is insightful. In many ways, Dreiser's work represents the opposite end of the spectrum from the romantic poets. For Stewart's use of the doctrine of original sin as a judgmental standard, see also Randall Stewart, *American Literature and Christian Doctrine* (Baton Rouge: Louisiana State University Press, 1958).

8. Clifton Fadiman, "Dreiser and the American Dream," *The Nation* 135 (19 October 1932): 364. Edward Wagenknecht contends that although Dreiser's reading of Spencer and Loeb influenced his work, it was his home environment that bordered on poverty that was the most important ingredient to his social concern. See Edward Wagenknecht, *Cavalcade of the American Novel: From the Birth of the Nation to the Middle of the Twentieth Century.* (New York: Holt, Rinehart and Winston, 1952), pp. 281–82. Furthermore, Grant Richards writes that the problems of Dreiser's characters personify his own personal struggles. Richards bases this assertion on an interview with Dreiser after *Jennie Gerhardt* was published. Dreiser mentioned problems with sex, prestige, and money as things that he must experience in order to write about them. See Grant Richards, *Author Hunting by An Old Literary Sports Man.* (New York: Coward McCann, Inc., 1934), pp. 176ff.

9. See Wesley A. Kort, *Narrative Elements and Religious Meanings.* (Philadelphia: Fortress Press, 1975). Kort's agenda involves approaching literature from the standpoint of the literary elements. Fictions are dominated by one or more of the elements while all four (atmosphere, character, plot, and tone) are always present. Narratives that are dominated by atmosphere approach the problem of limitations and possibilities that time and place and other aspects of atmosphere place upon the fictional world.

10. "The New York Times Saturday Review of Books," 15 June 1907, quoted in Ellen Moers, *Two Dreisers* (New York: The Viking Press, 1969), p. 184. Dreiser "was a seeker for ultimate truth, eager to investigate by every means the significance of the universe and man's relation to it. . . ." Dreiser's desire to find the truth prohibits one from classifying Dreiser by labels. His method varies as the

need for rational observation and description dictate in different circumstances. For the quote see J. D. Thomas, "The Natural Supernaturalism of Dreiser's Novels," *The Rice Institute Pamphlet* 44 (April 1957): 112–13. For a discussion on Dreiser's scientific method, see Woodburn O. Ross, "Concerning Dreiser's Mind," *American Literature* 18 (1946): 242 and Thomas, "The Natural Supernaturalism of Dreiser's Novels," p. 123, fn 10.

11. New York "Evening Sun," 18 June 1907, in Kazin, *The Stature of Theodore Dreiser,* p. 66.

12. Theodore Dreiser, as quoted in the "Foreword," *A Bibliography of the Writings of Theodore Dreiser* by Edward D. McDonald. (Philadelphia: The Centaur Book Shop, 1928), p. 12. See R. N. Mookerjee, *Theodore Dreiser: His Thought and Social Criticism.* (Delhi, India: National Publishing House, 1974), p. 1.

13. Russell Blankenship. *American Literature As An Expression of the National Mind.* (New York: Henry Holt and Company, 1931), pp. 538–40, and H. L. Mencken, *A Book of Prefaces.* (New York: Alfred A. Knopf, 1917), p. 88.

14. Randall Stewart, "Dreiser and the Naturalist Heresy," *The Virginia Quarterly Review* 34 (Winter 1958): 110–16. See also J. D. Thomas, "The Supernatural Naturalism of Dreiser's Novels," *The Rice Institute Pamphlet* 46 (April 1959): 68, fn 5.

15. George Snell, "Theodore Dreiser: Philosopher," *The Shapers of American Fiction* (New York: Cooper Square Publishers, Inc., 1961), p. 242 as quoted in Mookerjee, *Theodore Dreiser,* p. 51, fn 51. Mookerjee also quotes Dr. Sculley Bradley who said that Dreiser once told him that the famous lobster-squid passage (the most famous of his "survival of the fittest" passages) reflected Cowperwood's approach to life and not his own. See Mookerjee, *Theodore Dreiser,* p. 53–54. See also J. D. Thomas, "The Supernatural Naturalism of Dreiser's Novels," p. 53ff.

16. Kazin, "Introduction," p. 12. For a picture of Dreiser's life that illuminates his struggle with the problem of theodicy, see W. A. Swanberg, *Dreiser* (New York: Charles Scribner's Sons, 1965), pp. 41–45.

17. Theodore Dreiser, *Newspaper Days* (New York: Horace Liveright, 1922), pp. 65–66.

18. Theodore Dreiser, *An American Tragedy* (New York: New American Library, 1981), pp. 9, 23. See also pp. 512, 784; Theodore Dreiser, *The Stoic* (New York: The World Publishing Co., 1947), chap. 79 and the Appendix; and Theodore Dreiser, *The Titan* (New York: New American Library, 1965), pp. 18, 128, 168.

19. See Robert H. Elias, *Theodore Dreiser: Apostle of Nature* (New York: Alfred A. Knopf, 1949), p. ix for Dreiser as a dualistic writer. Gerald Willen solves the dualistic contradiction by asserting that Dreiser, the philosopher, writes about men and women who have no free will, while he creates fictional characters that are able to make choices. Thus, the dichotomy is not one within his thought. Rather, this dualism appears only as Dreiser changes discourse style from philosophy to narrative. See Gerald Willen, "Dreiser's Moral Seriousness." *University of Kansas City Review* 23 (Spring 1957): 181. See also F. O. Matthiessen, *Theodore Dreiser* (Scranton, Pa.: William Sloan Associates, 1951), p. 237; Moers, *Two Dreisers,* p. viii; and Donald Pizer, *The Novels of Theodore Dreiser: A Critical Study* (Minneapolis: University of Minnesota Press, 1976), p. 23, 5–25.

20. Charles Child Walcutt, "Theodore Dreiser and the Divided Stream," in Kazin, *The Stature of Theodore Dreiser,* p. 246.

21. Ibid., pp. 246–47.

22. For a discussion of pietism see David Brion Davis, "Dreiser and Naturalism Revisited," in Kazin, *The Stature of Theodore Dreiser.*

23. Blankenship, *American Literature As An Expression of the National Mind,* pp. 532–33.

24. Many critics discuss Dreiser's break with traditional literary designations and his qualified naturalism. For the best discussions see Kenneth S. Lynn, *Visions of America: Eleven Literary Historical Essays* (Westport, Conn.: Greenwood Press, 1973), pp. 140ff., Mookerjee, *Theodore Dreiser,* pp. 35ff., Thomas, "The Supernatural Naturalism," pp. 61–63, Thomas, "The Natural Supernaturalism," p. 118, and Wagenknecht, *Calvalcade of the American Novel,* pp. 281–84ff.

25. Theodore Dreiser, *Sister Carrie* (New York: New American Library, 1980), p. 74. See also Theodore Dreiser, *Dawn* (New York: Horace Liveright, 1931), p. 516.

26. Theodore Dreiser, *The Financier* (New York: New American Library, 1967), p. 8. See also pp. 240 and 446 for commentary on the instinct to survive.

27. Elias, *Theodore Dreiser: Apostle of Nature,* p. 164. For discussions on Dreiser's concept of the Superman and survival of the fittest, see also pp. 153–73; Pizer, *The Novels of Theodore Dreiser,* pp. 167ff; Matthiessen, *Theodore Dreiser,* p. 190; and Walcutt, "Theodore Dreiser and the Divided Stream," pp. 257ff.

28. Theodore Dreiser, *The Titan* (New York: New American Library, 1965), pp. 478, 425, chap. 20.

29. James T. Farrell, "Dreiser's *Sister Carrie,*" in Kazin, *The Stature of Theodore Dreiser,* p. 183 n.

30. Elias, *Theodore Dreiser: Apostle of Nature,* p. 120.

31. Ibid., pp. 209 and 283. See also Matthiessen, *Theodore Dreiser,* p. 205.

32. Moers, *Two Dreisers,* pp. 256–64; and Eliseo Vivas, "Dreiser, *An Inconsistent Mechanist,*" in Kazin, *The Stature of Theodore Dreiser,* pp. 238–39.

33. Robert Shafer, "*An American Tragedy:* A Humanistic Demurrer," in Kazin *The Stature of Theodore Dreiser,* p. 123.

34. Theodore Dreiser, *The Hand of the Potter* (New York: Boni and Liveright, 1918), p. 169. See also pp. 183–200.

35. Dreiser, *Sister Carrie,* chap. 33 and chap. 46. Especially p. 448.

36. Dreiser, *Newspaper Days,* p. 334. See also Shafer, *"An American Tragedy,"* p. 117.

37. Dreiser, *The Titan,* p. 56.

38. Theodore Dreiser, *The Stoic* (New York: The World Publishing Company, 1947), pp. 137, 197. See also *The Titan,* pp. 56, 145, 247, 289, and 500; Moers, *Two Dreisers,* pp. 228–42; and Shafer, *"An American Tragedy,"* pp. 115ff.

39. Dreiser, *The Financier,* pp. 268, 349, 51, 73; and *The Titan,* pp. 16, 59, 180, 407.

40. Dreiser, *Sister Carrie,* pp. 464–65.

41. Farrell, "Dreiser's *Sister Carrie,*" see note p. 183, 187.

42. George J. Becker, "Theodore Dreiser: The Realist as Social Critic," *Twentieth Century Literature: A Scholarly and Critical Journal* 1 (October 1955): 126. Mookerjee, *Theodore Dreiser,* p. 37. See also Lynn, *Visions of America,* p. 143, and Muller, *Modern Fiction: A Study of Values,* pp. 213ff. for discussions of Dreiser as a social critic.

43. Willen, "Dreiser's Moral Seriousness," pp. 182–87. Dreiser describes this conflict between society and personal ambition in Theodore Dreiser, "Neurotic America and the Sex Impulse," *Hey, Rub-A-Dub-Dub: A Book of the Mystery and Wonder and Terror of Life* (New York: Boni and Liveright, 1920), pp. 126–41. In

this article Dreiser discusses the senseless suppression of natural impulses by society. Such suppression works against natural law and creates social perversion
and misfits. His solution to this conflict between the natural and the social is to
let "Nature Herself" make laws, not society. (p. 141)

44. Theodore Dreiser, *Jennie Gerhardt* (New York: Schocken Books, 1982), pp.
360, 325.

45. Kazin, *An American Procession*, p. 241. Granville Hicks, "Theodore Dreiser," *The American Mercury* 62 (June 1946): 751. For the necessity of a new moral
system, see Kazin, *An American Procession*, p. 243 and Larzer Ziff, *The American
1890s: Life and Times of a Lost Generation* (New York: The Viking Press, 1966),
p. 338.

46. Fadiman, "Dreiser and the American Dream," p. 365. Mookerjee, *Theodore
Dreiser*, p. 88. See also Dreiser, *Tragic America*, pp. 247ff. for his critique of the
church.

47. Mookerjee, *Theodore Dreiser*, pp. 93–94. See also pp. 90, 113; and Becker,
"Theodore Dreiser: the Realist as Social Critic," p. 124–25.

48. Mookerjee, *Theodore Dreiser*, p. 113.

49. Ziff, *The American 1890s*, p. 336.

50. David W. Noble, "Dreiser and Veblen and the Literature of Cultural
Change," in Joseph J. Kwiat and Mary C. Turpie, eds., *Studies in American Culture:
Dominant Ideas and Images* (Minneapolis: University of Minnesota Press, 1960),
pp. 148–49.

51. Arvin Newton, "An American Case History," *New Republic* 67 (August
1931): 320; and Becker, "Theodore Dreiser: The Realist as Social Critic," pp.
120–23.

52. J. D. Thomas, "The Supernatural Naturalism of Dreiser's Novels," p. 66.

53. Theodore Dreiser, "A Lesson from the Aquarium," *Tom Watson's Magazine*
3 (January, 1906): 306–8.

54. For Dreiser's hostile attitude to the capitalistic system see Theodore Dreiser, *A Hoosier Holiday* (New York: John Lane Company, 1916), pp. 171–72; Dreiser, *America is Worth Saving* (New York: Modern Age Books, 1941); Dreiser,
Dreiser Looks at Russia (New York: H. Liveright, 1928); Dreiser, *Tragic America*
(New York: H. Liveright, 1931), pp. 30ff.; Dreiser, "Introduction," *Harlan Miners Speak* (New York: Harcourt, Brace and Company, 1932); Walter Blackstock,
"Dreiser's Dramatizations of American Success," *Florida State University Studies* 14
(1954): 107–30; John K. Huth, Jr., "Theodore Dreiser, Success Monger," *Colophon* 3 (Winter, 1938): 120–33; John F. Huth, Jr., "Dreiser and Success: An Additional Note," *Colophon* 3 (Summer, 1938): 406–10; and Mookerjee, *Theodore
Dreiser*, pp. 28, 50, 120ff., 136, 137.

55. See Granville Hicks, "Theodore Dreiser," p. 753; Ziff, *The American 1890s*,
pp. 339–43; and Kenneth Lynn, *Visions of America*, p. 142.

56. Wesley A. Kort, *Modern Fiction and Human Time: An Essay in Narrative and
Belief* (Tampa: University of South Florida Press, 1985), p. 10.

57. Thomas, "The Supernatural Naturalism of Dreiser's Novels," p. 59.
Kenny J. Williams points out Dreiser's ambiguous view of the city in her work
on Chicago. Chicago "is a *magnet* drawing [Carrie] into its electrifying circle. Neither can one forget Dreiser's later city which is composed of *titans* who answer
only the law of themselves." See Kenny J. Williams, *Prairie Voices: A Literary History of Chicago from the Frontier to 1893* (Nashville, Tenn.: Townsend Press, 1980),
p. 12; and Kenny J. Williams, *In the City of Men: Another Story of Chicago* (Nashville, Tenn.: Townsend Press, 1974), p. 388.

58. Theodore Dreiser, "The Loneliness of the City," *Tom Watson's Magazine* 2 (October 1905): 474–75. See also Fay M. Blake, *The Strike in the American Novel* (Metuchen, N.J.: The Scarecrow Press, 1972), pp. 83–85. Blake discusses the negative aspects of the city from the standpoint of labor and labor strikes. Blake is concerned with *Sister Carrie* and with the fall of Hurstwood as it relates to the streetcar strike that Dreiser describes in that novel.

59. Davis, "Dreiser and Naturalism Revisited," p. 234.

60. Muller, *Modern Fiction: A Study of Values*, pp. 208–11. Muller, like many other scholars, waver as to whether Dreiser is or is not a strict mechanist. My examination of his fiction reveals that Dreiser's philosophy and moral concern deliver him from the ranks of the purely mechanistic naturalists. Rather, his search for truth and meaning in life lies at the heart of his work. See also, Thomas, "The Supernatural Naturalism of Dreiser's Novels," pp. 61–63.

61. Davis, "Dreiser and Naturalism Revisited," pp. 226–32.

62. See Granville Hicks, "Theodore Dreiser and *The Bulwark;* and Lionel Trilling, "Reality in America," both in Kazin, *The Stature of Theodore Dreiser.* Hicks views *The Bulwark* as totally divorced from Dreiser's earlier work. In fact, for Hicks, *The Bulwark* is in opposition to Dreiser's naturalistic pieces, and it represents "the death knell of literary naturalism." See Hicks, "Theodore Dreiser," p. 755ff. I prefer to see *The Bulwark* as a complementary work to the rest of the Dreiser corpus.

63. Davis, "Dreiser and Naturalism Revisited," p. 236.

64. Theodore Dreiser, *The Bulwark* (Garden City, N.Y.: Doubleday and Company, 1946), p. 331.

65. Ibid.

66. Ibid., p. 319. See also Pizer, *Dreiser,* pp. 324ff.

67. Gerhard Friedrich, "A Major Influence on Theodore Dreiser's *The Bulwark,*" *American Literature* 29 (May 1957): 193. See also Gerhard Friedrich, "Theodore Dreiser's Debt to Woolman's *Journal,*" *American Quarterly* 7 (Winter 1955): 385–92. Friedrich's work arises out of a detailed comparative analysis between *The Bulwark* and Jones's writings. He isolates many thematic parallels as well as plot similarities between *The Bulwark* and John Woolman's life.

68. Friedrich, "A Major Influence on Theodore Dreiser's *The Bulwark,*" p. 183.

69. Ibid., pp. 183–88.

70. Ibid.

71. Ibid., p. 188.

72. See Friedrich, "Theodore Dreiser's Debt to Woolman's *Journal.*"

73. Carroll T. Brown, "Dreiser's *Bulwark* and Philadelphia Quakerism," *Bulletin of Friends Historical Association* 35 (Autumn 1946): pp. 52–54. See also Friedrich, "A Major Influence," pp. 189–90.

74. Brown, Dreiser's *Bulwark,*" pp. 61, 60.

75. Friedrich, "A Major Influence," p. 191.

76. See Moers, *Two Dreisers,* p. 230; and Hicks, "Theodore Dreiser and *The Bulwark,*" p. 221 for a discussion of the automobile and the city as the "antinatural."

77. Shuji Yamamoto, "Religion of Dreiser: Its Four Aspects," *Kyushu American Literature* 10 (December 1967): 70–71; and Marguerite Tjader, *Theodore Dreiser: A New Dimension* (Norwalk, Conn.: Silvermine Publishing Company, 1965), p. 127.

78. Noble, *The Eternal Adam and the New World Garden,* p. 132; Theodore Dreiser, *The "Genius",* (New York: World Publishing Company, 1946), p. 698;

Thomas, "The Supernatural Naturalism of Dreiser's Novels," pp. 56–57; and Thomas, "The Natural Supernaturalism of Dreiser's Novels," p. 114.

79. Dreiser, *The Bulwark,* pp. 318–19, 331, and chap. 66; Dustin Heustin, "Theodore Dreiser: Naturalist or Theist," *Brigham Young University Studies* 3 (Winter 1961): 45–47; and Friedrich, "Theodore Dreiser's Debt to Woolman's *Journal,*" p. 390.

80. Dreiser, "The Loneliness of the City," p. 475.

81. Pizer, *Dreiser,* p. 337.

82. Dreiser, *The Stoic,* p. 306.

83. See Vivas, "Dreiser, An Inconsistent Mechanist," pp. 243–44 for an example of this viewpoint. See also Jane Benardete, *American Realism* (New York: G. P. Putnam's Sons, 1972), pp. 17ff.

84. See Mookerjee, *Theodore Dreiser,* pp. 35ff., and Thomas, "The Natural Supernaturalism of Dreiser's Novels," pp. 116ff.

85. Ford Madox Ford, "Portrait of Dreiser," in Kazin *The Stature of Theodore Dreiser,* pp. 33–34.

86. Ibid.

87. Shafer, *"An American Tragedy,"* p. 122.

88. For the uselessness of traditional moral codes, see Lynn, *Visions of America,* p. 140; Shafer, *"An American Tragedy,"* p. 121; and Walcutt, "Theodore Dreiser and the Divided Stream," pp. 251ff. For the rebellion theme, see Hicks, "Theodore Dreiser and *The Bulwark,*" p. 220. For the comment on the genteel tradition, see Malcolm Cowley, "Sister Carrie: Her Fall and Rise," in Kazin, *The Stature of Theodore Dreiser,* p. 176.

89. Ellen Moers points out the connection by referring to *Dawn.* See Moers, *Two Dreisers,* pp. 292–302. Helen Dreiser also comments upon the important role that religious fanaticism plays in Dreiser's conception of *An American Tragedy.* See Helen Dreiser, *My Life With Dreiser* (New York: World Publishing Company, 1951), pp. 34–37.

90. Shafer, *"An American Tragedy,"* p. 122.

91. Dreiser, *An American Tragedy,* pp. 9, 13, 16, 249, 445, 623, 625, 778, 784, and 800.

92. Ibid., p. 814.

93. Pizer, *The Novels of Theodore Dreiser,* pp. 144, 58, 191ff.

94. See Wesley A. Kort, *Moral Fiber: Character and Belief in Recent American Fiction* (Philadelphia: Fortress Press, 1982), especially part 3 for a development of Kort's understanding of the visionary character in fiction. It is this usage of "visionary" that I employ here.

95. Dreiser, *Jennie Gerhardt,* p. 82.

96. Vivas, "Dreiser, An Inconsistent Mechanist," p. 243, and Thomas, "The Natural Supernaturalism of Dreiser's Novels," p. 118.

97. Dreiser, *The Bulwark,* p. 328.

98. Dreiser, *Jennie Gerhardt,* p. 367.

Chapter 4. A New American Dream

1. See Wesley A. Kort, *Narrative Elements and Religious Meaning* (Philadelphia: Fortress Press, 1975), pp. 20–39; and Kort, *Moral Fiber: Character and Belief in Recent American Fiction* (Philadelphia: Fortress Press, 1982), p. 3.

2. I am indebted to the work of Paul Ricoeur and to my many discussions

with Wesley Kort concerning Ricoeur for the development of this hermeneutical principle. See especially Paul Ricoeur, *The Conflict of Interpretations: Essays in Hermeneutics,* ed. Don Ihde (Evanston, Ill.: Northwestern University Press, 1974).

3. The word "estrangers" is used by John Eddins in his systematic theology to describe the person estranged from God. Lecture in Systemic Theology, Spring 1981, Southeastern Baptist Theological Seminary. I use this term to describe the nineteenth-century American situated in an alien environment. However, this term also applies to anyone who experiences dislocation or marginality as these terms are used in this study.

4. See Catherine Albanese, *America: Religions and Religion* (Belmont, Calif.: Wadsworth Publishing Company, 1981), pp. 283–309.

5. See Herbert J. Muller, Modern Fiction: A Study of Values (New York: Funk and Wagnalls, 1937), p. 22.

6. For Chopin's *The Awakening,* see Per Seyersted, *Kate Chopin: A Critical Biography* (New York: Octagon Books, 1980); and Peggy Skaggs, *Kate Chopin* (Boston: Twayne Publishers, 1985). For Twain's *Adventures of Huckleberry Finn,* see Walter Blair, *Mark Twain and Huck Finn* (Berkeley: University of California Press, 1960); Louis J. Budd, *Mark Twain: Social Philosopher* (Bloomington: Indiana University Press, 1962); Philip S. Foner, *Mark Twain, Social Critic* (New York: International Publishers 1958); Henry Nash Smith, *Mark Twain's Fable of Progress: Political and Economic Ideas in "A Connecticut Yankee"* (New Brunswick, N.J.: Rutgers University Press, 1964); and Edward Wagenknecht, *Mark Twain, The Man and His Work,* rev. ed. (Norman: University of Oklahoma Press, 1961).

7. For Crane's *The Red Badge of Courage,* see Maurice Bassan, ed. *Stephen Crane: A Collection of Critical Essays* (Englewood Cliffs, N.J.: Prentice-Hall, 1967); Edwin H. Cady, *Stephen Crane* (New York: Twayne, 1962); Joseph Katz, ed. *Stephen Crane in Transition: Centenary Essays* (DeKalb: Northern Illinois University Press, 1972); Donald Pizer, "Stephen Crane," in *Fifteen American Authors Before 1900: Bibliographic Essays on Research and Criticism,* ed. by Robert A. Rees and Earl N. Harbert (Madison: University of Wisconsin Press, 1971), pp. 97–138; and Eric Solomon, *Stephen Crane: From Parody to Realism* (Cambridge: Harvard University Press, 1966. For Wharton's *Ethan Frome* see Elizabeth Ammons, *Edith Wharton's Argument with America* (Athens: University of Georgia Press, 1980); Irving Howe, ed., *Edith Wharton: A Collection of Critical Essays* (Englewood Cliffs, N.J.: Prentice Hall, 1962); and Geoffrey Walton, *Edith Wharton: A Critical Interpretation* (Rutherford, N.J.: Fairleigh Dickinson University Press, 1974).

8. Giles Gunn, *The Interpretation of Otherness: Literature, Religion, and the American Imagination* (New York: Oxford University Press, 1979), pp. 187, 171.

9. Mircea Eliade, *The Sacred and the Profane: The Nature of Religion* Trans. Willard R. Trask (New York: Harcourt Brace Jovanovich, 1959), p. 4.

10. Ibid., p. 14.

11. Lynn Ross-Bryant, *Imagination and the Life of the Spirit: An Introduction to the Study of Religion and Literature,* (Chico, Calif.: Scholars Press, 1981), p. 16. Lynn Ross-Bryant cites Gilkey's four characteristics of secularity from *Naming the Whirlwind: The Renewal of God-Language* in delinating her picture of secularity in the modern world. These four characteristics follow:

1. The first characteristic of secularity is contingency. Contingency describes the attitude that there is no necessity for things to be—things are not a part of a divine plan. Rather, "things simply are."

2. Relativity describes the second characteristic of secularity and speaks to the lack of absolutes in the modern world.

3. Temporality is the third characteristic of secularity and takes on the form of change in the modern scheme of time. Change is thus fundamental to the secularizing influence of the modern world.

4. The fourth characteristic of secularity is autonomy. Independence and freedom from the transcendent and responsibility for events in the world are key to the secularizing movement.

For these characteristics, see Ross-Bryant *Imagination and the Life of the Spirit*, p. 17. See also Langdon Gilkey, *Naming the Whirlwind: The Renewal of God-Language* (Indianapolis, Ind.: Bobbs-Merrill Company, 1969).

It is interesting to note that these four characteristics are prominent themes in the fiction of Theodore Dreiser and Willa Cather. Cather and Dreiser both inherited and helped to generate the move to secular attitudes in America. One manifestation of this secularization occurs in the conception of space that each author develops. One purpose of this study is to describe how these and other characteristics of secularity operate through fictional conceptions of space in order to redefine the meaning of space.

12. J. Hillis Miller, *Poets of Reality: Six Twentieth Century Writers* (New York: Atheneum, 1974), p. 2.

13. Ibid., pp. 5ff.

14. George M. Marsden, *Fundamentalism and American Culture: The Shaping of Twentieth-Century Evangelicalism 1870–1925* (Oxford: Oxford University Press, 1980), pp. 5–6. Marsden's treatment of fundamentalism views the movement as a legitimate religious movement without neglecting the interplay between the movement and its beliefs and cultural forces and conditions.

15. See Donald G. Mathews, *Religion in the Old South* (Chicago: University of Chicago Press, 1977); and Robert Mapes Anderson, *Vision of the Disinherited: The Making of American Pentecostalism* (New York: Oxford University Press, 1979). Mathew's method involves the reconstruction of popular culture and grass roots religion. He often assumes a conflictual model for his reconstruction of Southern evangelicalism, and religion is an agent of social change and redefinition. Robert Mapes Anderson operates from a similar methodological perspective in *Vision of the Disinherited*. Both approaches rely partially upon a Marxist understanding of religion, and they assume a functional definition for religious experience—i.e., religion acts to ensure social and psychological wholeness. It is this functional understanding of religion without the Marxist implications it brings that I claim for this project.

16. A. J. Greimas understands dramatic narrative in "before" and "after" terms that result in the "reversal of the situation." The "after" situation involves a movement toward completion and toward the re-establishment of a ruptured social contract. The narrative body accommodates the movement from the disruption of a social norm to the re-establishment of social acceptability. See Greimas, "The Interpretation of Myth: Theory and Practice" in *Structural Analysis of Oral Tradition*, ed. Pierre Maranda and Elli Kongas Maranda (Philadelphia: University of Pennsylvania Press, 1971), p. 83, 81–121. Thus, at least one function of narrative is to provide legitimacy when dislocation occurs. See also Greimas, "Elements of a Narrative Grammar," translated by Catherine Porter, *Diacritics* 7 (March 1977): 23–40; *Semantique Structurale Recherche de Methode* (Paris: Librairie Larousse, 1966); and A. J. Greimas and J. Courtes, "The Cognitive Dimension of Narrative Discourse," *New Literary History* 7 (Spring 1976): 433–47.

17. Clifford Geertz, "Thick Description: Toward an Interpretive Theory of Culture," in *The Interpretation of Cultures: Selected Essays* (New York: Basic Books, Inc., 1973), p. 5.

18. Ibid., p. 30.

19. Peter L. Berger, *The Sacred Canopy: Elements of a Sociological Theory of Religion* (Garden City, N.Y.: Doubleday and Co., Inc., 1967), p. 4.

20. Ibid., pp. 47 and 180.

21. Ibid., p. 29.

22. Peter L.Berger and Thomas Luckmann, *The Social Construction of Reality: A Treatise in the Sociology of Knowledge* (Garden City, N.Y.: Doubleday and Co., Inc., 1966), p. 92.

23. Berger, *The Sacred Canopy*, p. 32.

24. Greimas, *Semantique Structurale*, p. 213.

Select Bibliography

Willa Cather

PRIMARY SOURCES

Cather, Willa. *Alexander's Bridge.* Boston: Houghton Mifflin, 1912.

———. *Death Comes For the Archbishop.* New York: Vintage Books, 1971. Originally published by Alfred A. Knopf, Inc., 1927.

———. *A Lost Lady.* New York: Vintage Books, 1972. Originally published by Alfred A. Knopf, Inc., 1923.

———. *My Ántonia.* Boston: Houghton Mifflin, 1949. Originally published in 1918.

———. *My Mortal Enemy.* New York: Vintage Books, 1954. Originally published by Alfred A. Knopf, Inc., 1926.

———. *O Pioneers!* Boston: Houghton Mifflin, 1913.

———. *Obscure Destinies.* New York: Vintage Books, 1974. Originally published by Alfred A. Knopf, Inc., 1932.

———. *One of Ours.* New York: Vintage Books, 1971. Originally published by Alfred A. Knopf, Inc., 1922.

———. *The Professor's House.* London: Hamish Hamilton, 1961. Originally published by Alfred A. Knopf, Inc., 1925.

———. *The Song of the Lark.* Boston: Houghton Mifflin, 1915.

———. *Youth and the Bright Medusa.* New York: Vintage Books, 1975. Originally published by Alfred A. Knopf, Inc., 1920.

SECONDARY SOURCES

Books

Alderman Library. *Miracles of Perception: The Art of Willa Cather.* Charlottesville: University of Virginia, 1980.

Arnold, Marilyn. *Willa Cather's Short Fiction.* Athens: Ohio University Press, 1984.

Bennett, Mildred. *The World of Willa Cather.* New York: Dodd, Mead and Company, 1951.

Bloom, Edward A., and Lillian D. Bloom. *Willa Cather's Gift of Sympathy.* Carbondale: Southern Illinois University Press, 1962.

Brown, E. K. Completed by Leon Edel. *Willa Cather: A Critical Biography.* New York: Alfred A. Knopf, Inc., 1953.

Daiches, David. *Willa Cather: A Critical Introduction.* Ithaca: Cornell University Press, 1951.

Giannone, Richard. *Music in Willa Cather's Fiction*. Lincoln: University of Nebraska Press, 1968.

Murphy, John J., ed. *Critical Essays on Willa Cather*. Boston: G. K. Hall and Company, 1984.

————, ed. *Five Essays on Willa Cather: The Merrimack Symposium*. North Andover, Mass.: Merrimack College, 1974.

Randall, John H., III. *The Landscape and the Looking Glass: Willa Cather's Search for Value*. Boston: Houghton Mifflin, 1960.

Rapin, Rene. *Willa Cather*. Vol. 8: *Modern American Writers*. Edited by Ernest Boyd. New York: R. M. McBride and Company, 1930.

Robinson, Phyllis C. *Willa: The Life of Willa Cather*. Garden City, N.Y.: Doubleday and Company, 1983.

Schroeter, James. *Willa Cather and Her Critics*. Ithaca: Cornell University Press, 1967.

Shively, James R. *Writings From Willa Cather's Campus Years*. Lincoln: University of Nebraska Press, 1950.

Stouck, David. *Willa Cather's Imagination*. Lincoln: University of Nebraska Press, 1975.

Van Ghent, Dorothy. *Willa Cather*. Minneapolis: University of Minnesota Press, 1964.

Articles

Adams, Theodore S. "Willa Cather's *My Mortal Enemy:* The Concise Presentation of Scene, Character, and Theme." *Colby Library Quarterly* 10 (September 1973): 138–48.

Baum, Bernard. "Willa Cather's Waste Land." *The South Atlantic Quarterly* 48 (October 1949): 589–601.

Bloom, Edward A., and Lillian D. Bloom. "Willa Cather's Novels of the Frontier: A Study in Thematic Symbolism." *American Literature* 21 (March 1949): 71–93.

Charles, Sister Peter Damian, O. P. "Love and Death in Willa Cather's *O Pioneers!*" *CLA Journal* 9 (December 1965): 140–50.

Cooper, Frederick Taber. "Review of *O Pioneers!*." In *Critical Essays on Willa Cather*, edited by John J. Murphy, pp. 112–13. Boston: G. K. Hall and Company, 1984.

Earnest, Ernest. "The American Ariel." *The South Atlantic Quarterly* 45 (Spring 1966): 192–200.

Ferguson, J. M., Jr. "'Vague Outlines': Willa Cather's Enchanted Bluffs." *Western Review* 7 (Spring 1970): 61–64.

Fisher, Dorothy Canfield. "Review of *Sapphira and the Slave Girl*." In *Critical Essays on Willa Cather*, edited by John J. Murphy, pp. 284–86. Boston: G. K. Hall and Company, 1984. Originally in *Book-of-the-Month Club News* (December 1940): 2–3.

Forman, Henry James. "Willa Cather: A Voice from the Prairie." *Southwest Review* 47 (Summer 1962): 248–58.

Fox, Maynard. "Proponents of Order: Tom Outland and Bishop Latour." *Western American Literature* 4 (Summer 1969): 107–15.

Fryer, Judith. "Cather's Felicitous Space." *Prairie Schooner* 55 (Spring/Summer 1981): 185–98.

Geismar, Maxwell. "Willa Cather: Lady in the Wilderness." In *Willa Cather and Her Critics,* edited by James Schroeter, pp. 171–202. Ithaca: Cornell University Press, 1967. Reprinted from *The Last of the Provincials.* Boston: Houghton Mifflin, 1947.

Hicks, Granville. "The Case Against Willa Cather." In *Willa Cather and Her Critics,* edited by James Schroeter, pp. 139–47. Ithaca: Cornell University Press, 1967. Reprinted from the *English Journal* (November 1933).

Jobes, Lavon Mattes. "Willa Cather's Last Novel." *The University Review* 34 (October 1967): 77–80.

Kazin, Alfred. "Willa Cather." In *Willa Cather and Her Critics,* edited by James Schroeter, pp. 161–70. New York: Cornell University Press, 1967. Reprinted from *On Native Grounds.* New York: Harcourt, Brace, and World, Inc., 1942.

Mencken, H. L. "Review of *One of Ours.*" In *Willa Cather and Her Critics,* edited by James Schroeter, pp. 7–12. Ithaca: Cornell University Press, 1967. Reprinted from the *Smart Set* (January 1916).

Miller, James E., Jr. "The Nebraska Encounter: Willa Cather and Wright Morris." *Prairie Schooner* 41 (Summer 1967): 165–67.

Murphy, John J. "A Comprehensive View of Cather's *O Pionners!.*" In *Critical Essays on Willa Cather,* edited by John J. Murphy, pp. 113–27. Boston: G. K. Hall and Company, 1984.

———. "Cooper, Cather, and the Downward Path to Progress." *Prairie Schooner* 55 (Spring/Summer 1981): 168–84.

———. "Willa Cather: The Widening Gyre." In *Five Essays on Willa Cather: The Merrimack Symposium,* edited by John J. Murphy, pp. 51–74. North Andover, Mass.: Merrimack College, 1974.

Murphy, John J. and Synnott, Kevin A. "Introduction." In *Critical Essays on Willa Cather,* edited by John J. Murphy, pp. 1–28. Boston: G. K. Hall and Company, 1984.

Randall, John H., III. "Willa Cather and the Pastoral Tradition." In *Five Essays on Willa Cather: The Merrimack Symposium,* edited by John J. Murphy, pp. 75–96. North Andover, Mass.: Merrimack College, 1974.

Schneider, Sister Lucy, C.S.J. "Artistry and Instinct: Willa Cather's 'Land-Philosophy'." *College Language Association Journal* 16 (June 1973): 485–504.

———. "Cather's 'Land-Philosophy' in *Death Comes for the Archbishop.*" *Renascence* 22 (Winter 1970): 78–86.

Schneider, Sister Lucy, C. S. J. "*O Pioneers!* in the Light of Willa Cather's 'Land-Philosophy'." *Colby Library Quarterly* 8 (June 1968): 55–70.

———. "Willa Cather's Early Stories in the Light of Her 'Land-Philosophy'." *The Midwest Quarterly* 9 (October 1967): 75–94.

Slote, Berenice. "Willa Cather: The Secret Web." In *Five Essays on Willa Cather: The Merrimack Symposium,* edited by John J. Murphy, pp. 1–19. North Andover, Mass.: Merrimack College, 1974.

Sullivan, Patrick J. "Willa Cather's Southwest." *Western American Literature* 7 (Spring 1972): 25–37.

Trilling, Lionel. "Willa Cather." In *Willa Cather and Her Critics,* edited by James Schroeter, pp. 148–55. Ithaca: Cornell University Press, 1967. Originally published in the *New Republic.* Also in Cowley, Malcolm, ed. *After the Genteel Tradition: American Writers: 1910–1930.* Carbondale: Southern Illinois University Press, 1937.

Welty, Eudora. "The House of Willa Cather." In *Miracles of Perception: The Art of Willa Cather,* pp. 8–30. Alderman Library. Charlottesville: University of Virginia, 1980.

Wermuth, Paul C. "Willa Cather's Virginia Novel." *Virginia Cavalcade* 7 (Spring 1958): 4–7.

Yongue, Patricia Lee. "*A Lost Lady:* The End of the First Cycle." *Western American Literature* 7 (Spring 1972): 3–12.

Theodore Dreiser

PRIMARY SOURCES

Dreiser, Theodore. *America is Worth Saving.* New York: Modern Age Books, 1941.

———. *An American Tragedy.* New York: The New American Library, 1981. Originally published by Horace Liveright, Inc., 1925.

———. *The Bulwark.* Garden City, N.Y.: Doubleday and Company, 1946.

———. *Dawn.* New York: Horace Liveright, Inc., 1931.

———. *Dreiser Looks at Russia.* New York: Horace Liveright, Inc., 1928.

———. *The Financier.* New York: New American Library, 1967. Originally published by Harper and Brothers, 1912.

———. "Foreword." In *A Bibliography of the Writings of Theodore Dreiser,* compiled by Edward D. McDonald, pp. 11–12. Philadelphia: The Centaur Book Shop, 1928.

———. *Free, and Other Stories.* New York: Boni and Liveright, 1918.

———. *The "Genius".* New York: John Lane Company, 1915.

———. *The Hand of the Potter.* New York: Boni and Liveright, 1918.

———. *Hey-Rub-A-Dub-Dub: A Book of the Mystery and Wonder and Terror of Life.* New York: Boni and Liveright, 1920.

———. *A Hoosier Holiday.* New York: John Lane Company, 1916.

———. "Introduction," *Harlan Miners Speak.* New York: Harcourt, Brace and Company, 1932.

———. *Jennie Gerhardt.* New York: Schocken Books, 1982. Originally published by Harper and Brothers, 1911.

———. "A Lesson from the Aquarium." *Tom Watson's Magazine* 3 (January 1906): 306–8.

———. "The Loneliness of the City." *Tom Watson's Magazine* 2 (October 1905): 474–75.

———. *Newspaper Days.* New York: Horace Liveright, Inc., 1922.

———. *Sister Carrie.* New York: The New American Library, 1980. Originally published by Doubleday, 1900.

———. *The Stoic.* New York: The World Publishing Company, 1947.

———. *The Titan.* New York: The New American Library, 1965. Originally published by the John Lane Company, 1914.

———. *Tragic America.* New York: Horace Liveright, Inc., 1931.

SECONDARY SOURCES

Books

Blake, Fay M. *The Strike in the American Novel.* Metuchen, N.J.: The Scarecrow Press, Inc., 1972.

Dreiser, Helen. *My Life With Dreiser.* New York: World Publishing Company, 1951.

Elias, Robert H. *Theodore Dreiser: Apostle of Nature.* New York: Alfred A. Knopf, 1949.

Kazin, Alfred and Shapiro, Charles, eds. *The Stature of Theodore Dreiser.* Bloomington: Indiana University Press, 1955.

McDonald, Edward D. *A Bibliography of the Writings of Theodore Dreiser.* Philadelphia: The Centaur Book Shop, 1928.

Matthiessen, F. O. *Theodore Dreiser.* Scranton, Pa.: William Sloan Associates, Inc., 1951.

Mencken, H. L. *A Book of Prefaces.* New York: Alfred A. Knopf, 1917.

Moers, Ellen. *Two Dreisers.* New York: The Viking Press, 1969.

Mookerjee, R. N. *Theodore Dreiser: His Thought and Social Criticism.* Delhi, India: National Publishing House, 1974.

Pizer, Donald. *The Novels of Theodore Dreiser: A Critical Study.* Minneapolis: University of Minnesota Press, 1976.

Swanberg, W. A. *Dreiser.* New York: Charles Scribner's Sons, 1965.

Tjader, Marguerite. *Theodore Dreiser: A New Dimension:* Norwalk, Conn.: Silvermine Publishing, Inc., 1965.

Articles

Becker, George J. "Theodore Dreiser: The Realist as Social Critic." *Twentieth Century Literature: A Scholarly and Critical Journal* 1 (October 1955): 117–27.

Blackstock, Walter. "Dreiser's Dramatizations of American Success." *Florida State University Studies* 14 (1954): 107–30.

Brown, Carroll T. "Dreiser's *Bulwark* and Philadelphia Quakerism." *Bulletin of Friends Historical Association* 35 (Autumn 1946): 52–61.

Cowley, Malcolm. "Sister Carrie: Her Fall and Rise." In *The Stature of Theodore Dreiser,* edited by Alfred Kazin and Charles Shapiro, pp. 171–81. Bloomington: Indiana University Press, 1955.

Davis, David Brion. "Dreiser and Naturalism Revisited." In *The Stature of Theodore Dreiser,* edited by Alfred Kazin and Charles Shapiro, pp. 225–36. Bloomington: Indiana University Press, 1955.

Fadiman, Clifton. "Dreiser and the American Dream." *The Nation* 135 (19 October 1932): 364–65.

Farrell, James T. "Dreiser's *Sister Carrie.*" In *The Stature of Theodore Dreiser,* edited by Alfred Kazin and Charles Shapiro, pp. 182–87. Bloomington: Indiana University Press, 1955.

Ford, Ford Madox. "Portrait of Dreiser." In *The Stature of Theodore Dreiser,* edited by Alfred Kazin and Charles Shapiro, pp. 21–35. Bloomington: Indiana University Press, 1955.

Friedrich, Gerhard. "A Major Influence on Theodore Dreiser's *The Bulwark.*" *American Literature* 29 (May 1957): 180–93.

———. "Theodore Dreiser's Debt to Woolman's *Journal.*" *American Quarterly* 7 (Winter 1955): 385–92.

Heustin, Dustin. "Theodore Dreiser: Naturalist or Theist." *Brigham Young University Studies* 3 (Winter 1961): 41–49.

Hicks, Granville. "Theodore Dreiser." *The American Mercury* 62 (June 1946): 751–56.

———. "Theodore Dreiser and *The Bulwark.*" In *The Stature of Theodore Dreiser,* edited by Alfred Kazin and Charles Shapiro, pp. 219–24. Bloomington: Indiana University Press, 1955.

Huth, John F., Jr. "Dreiser and Success: An Additional Note." *Colophon* 3 (Summer 1983): 406–10.

———. "Theodore Dreiser, Success Monger." *Colophon* 3 (Winter 1938): 120–33.

"Newspaper Interview." *The New York Times Saturday Review of Books,* 15 June 1907, p. 393. Quoted in *Two Dreisers,* p. 184. By Ellen Moers. New York: The Viking Press, 1969.

"Newspaper Review." New York *Evening Sun,* 18 June 1907. In *The Stature of Theodore Dreiser,* p. 66. Edited by Alfred Kazin and Charles Shapiro. Bloomington: Indiana University Press, 1955.

Newton, Arvin. "An American Case History." *New Republic* 67 (5 August 1931): 319–20.

Noble, David W. "Dreiser and Veblen and the Literature of Cultural Change." In *Studies in American Culture: Dominant Ideas and Images,* edited by Joseph Kwiat and Mary C. Turpie, pp. 139–52. Minneapolis: University of Minnesota Press, 1960.

Ross, Woodburn O. "Concerning Dreiser's Mind." *American Literature* 18 (1946): 233–43.

Shafer, Robert. "*An Amedrican Tragedy:* A Humanistic Demurrer." In *The Stature of Theodore Dreiser,* edited by Alfred Kazin and Charles Shapiro, pp. 113–26. Bloomington: Indiana University Press, 1955.

Snell, George. "Theodore Dreiser: Philosopher." Chap. 18 in *The Shapers of American Fiction.* New York: Cooper Square Publishers, Inc.,1961.

Stewart, Randall. "Dreiser and the Naturalist Heresy." *Virginia Quarterly Review* 34 (Winter 1958): 100–16.

Thomas, J. D. "The Natural Supernaturalism of Dreiser's Novels." *The Rice Institute Pamphlet* 44 (April 1957): 112–25.

———. "The Supernatural Naturalism of Dreiser's Novels." *The Rice Institute Pamphlet* 46 (April 1959): 53–69.

Trilling, Lionel. "Reality in America." In *The Stature of Theodore Dreiser,* edited by Alfred Kazin and Charles Shapiro, pp. 132–45. Bloomington: Indiana University Press, 1955.

Vivas, Eliseo. "Dreiser, An Inconsistent Mechanist." In *The Stature of Theodore Dreiser,* edited by Alfred Kazin and Charles Shapiro, pp. 237–45. Bloomington: Indiana University Press, 1955.

Walcutt, Charles Child. "Theodore Dreiser and the Divided Stream." In *The Stature of Theodore Dreiser,* edited by Alfred Kazin and Charles Shapiro, pp. 246–69. Bloomington: Indiana University Press, 1955.

Willen, Gerald. "Dreiser's Moral Seriousness." *University of Kansas City Review* 23 (Spring 1957): 181–87.

Yamamoto, Shuji. "Religion of Dreiser: Its Four Aspects." *Kyushu American Literature* 10 (December 1967): 70–74.

Literary, Cultural, and Religious Studies

Abrams, M. H. *Natural Supernaturalism.* New York: W. W. Norton and Company, 1971.

Ahnebrink, Lars. *The Beginnings of Naturalism in American Fiction: A Study of the Works of Hamlin Garland, Stephen Crane, and Frank Norris with Special Reference to Some European Influences: 1891–1903.* Essays and Studies on American Language and Literature, vol. 9. New York: Russell and Russell, Inc., 1961.

Albanese, Catherine. *America: Religions and Religion.* Belmont, Calif.: Wadsworth Publishing Company, 1981.

Anderson, Robert Mapes. *Vision of the Disinherited: The Making of American Pentecostalism.* New York: Oxford University Press, 1979.

Bachelard, Gaston. *The Poetics of Space.* Translated by Etienne Gilson. Boston: Beacon Press, 1969.

Bauer-Yocum, Timothy S. "In Search of a Myth for Modern America: Spiritual and Cultural Renewal in Walt Whitman and Henry Adams." Ph.D. diss., Duke University, 1983.

Benardete, Jane. *American Realism.* New York: G. P. Putman's Sons, 1972.

Bercovitch, Sacvan. *The American Jeremiad.* Madison: University of Wisconsin Press, 1978.

Berger, Peter. *The Sacred Canopy: Elements of a Sociological Theory of Religion.* Garden City, N.Y.: Doubleday and Company, Inc., 1967.

Berger, Peter, and Luckmann, Thomas. *The Social Construction of Reality: A Treatise in the Sociology of Knowledge.* Garden City, N.Y.: Doubleday and Company, Inc., 1966.

Blankenship, Russell. *American Literature As An Expression of the National Mind.* New York: Henry Holt and Company, 1931.

Brown, E. K. *Rhythm in the Novel.* Toronto: University of Toronto Press, 1950.

Canby, Henry Seidel, ed. *The Works of Thoreau.* Boston: Houghton Mifflin, 1937.

Carroll, Peter N. *Puritanism and the Wilderness: The Intellectual Significance of the New England Frontier, 1629–1700.* New York: Columbia University Press, 1969.

Cowley, Malcolm, ed. *After the Genteel Tradition: American Writers: 1910–1930.* Carbondale: Southern Illinois Press, 1937.

Eliade, Mircea. *The Sacred and the Profane: The Nature of Religion.* Translated by Willard R. Trask. New York: Harcourt Brace Jovanovich, 1959.

Ellman, Richard and Feidelson, Charles, Jr. *The Modern Tradition: Backgrounds of Modern Literature.* New York: Oxford University Press, 1965.

Geertz, Clifford. *The Interpretation of Cultures: Selected Essays.* New York: Basic Books, Inc., 1973.

Gilkey, Langdon. *Naming the Whirlwind: The Renewal of God Language.* Indianapolis, Ind.: Bobbs-Merrill, 1969.

Goodin, George. *The English Novel in the Nineteenth Century: Essays on the Literary Mediation of Human Values*. Chicago: University of Illinois Press, 1972.

Greimas, A. J. "Elements of a Narrative Grammar." Translated by Catherine Porter. *Diacritics* 7 (March 1977): 23–40.

———. *Semantique Structurale Recherche de Methode*. Paris: Librairie Larousse, 1966.

———. *Structural Analysis of Oral Tradition*. Edited by Pierre Maranda and Elli Kongas Maranda. Philadelphia: Univerity of Pennsylvania Press, 1971.

Greimas, A. J. and Courtes, J. "The Cognitive Dimension of Narrative Discourse." *New Literary History* (Spring 1976): 433–47.

Gunn, Giles. *New World Metaphysics: Readings on the Religious Meaning of the American Experience*. New York: Oxford University Press, 1981.

———. *The Interpretation of Otherness: Literature, Religion, and the American Imagination*. New York: Oxford University Press, 1979.

Hicks, John D. *The Populist Revolt*. Nebraska: University of Nebraska Press, 1961.

Holloway, Mark. *Heavens on Earth: Utopian Communities in America 1680–1880*. London: Tunstile Press, 1951.

Hutchison, William R. *The Modernist Impulse in American Protestantism*. Cambridge: Harvard University Press, 1976.

Jones, Howard Mumford. *The Frontier in American Fiction*. Jerusalem: The Magness Press, 1956.

Kazin, Alfred. *An American Procession: The Major Writers from 1830–1930—The Crucial Century*. New York: Vintage Books, Random House, 1984.

———. *On Native Grounds: An Interpretation of Modern American Prose Literature*. New York: Harcourt, Brace and World, Inc., 1942.

Kort, Wesley A. *Modern Fiction and Human Time: An Essay in Narrative and Belief*. Tampa: University of South Florida Press, 1985.

———. *Moral Fiber: Character and Belief in Recent American Fiction*. Philadelphia: Fortress Press, 1982.

———. *Narrative Elements and Religious Meaning*. Philadelphia: Fortress Press, 1975.

Kwiat, Joseph J. and Turpie, Mary C., eds. *Studies in American Culture: Dominant Ideas and Images*. Minneapolis: University of Minnesota Press, 1960.

Lee, Robert Edson. *From West to East: Studies in the Literature of the American West*. Urbana: University of Illinois Press, 1966.

Lemon, Lee T. "The Hostile Universe: A Developing Pattern in Nineteenth-Century Fiction." In *The English Novel in the Nineteenth Century: Essays on the Literary Mediation of Human Values*, edited by George Goodin. Chicago: University of Illinois Press, 1972.

Lewis, R. W. B. *Trials of the Word*. New Haven: Yale University Press, 1965.

Lynn, Kenneth S. *Visions of America: Eleven Literary Historical Essays*. Westport, Conn.: Greenwood Press, Inc., 1973.

Marsden, George M. *Fundamentalism and American Culture: The Shaping of Twentieth-Century Evangelicalism 1870–1925*. Oxford: Oxford University Press, 1980.

Marx, Leo. *Machine in the Garden*. New York: Oxford University Press, 1964.

Mathews, Donald G. *Religion in the Old South.* Chicago: The University of Chicago Press, 1977.

Miller, J. Hillis. *Poets of Reality: Six Twentieth Century Writers.* New York: Atheneum, 1974.

Miller, Perry, ed. *American Thought: Civil War to World War I.* New York: Rinehart and Company, Inc., 1954.

————. *Errand Into the Wilderness.* Cambridge: Harvard University Press, 1956.

Monroe, Elizabeth. *The Novel and Society.* Chapel Hill: University of North Carolina Press, 1941.

Muller, Herbert J. *Modern Fiction: A Study of Values.* New York: Funk and Wagnalls Company, 1937.

Noble, David W. *The Eternal Adam and the New World Garden: The Central Myth in the American Novel Since 1830.* New York: Braziller, 1968.

Otto, Rudolf. *The Idea of the Holy: An Inquiry Into the Non-Rational Factor in the Idea of the Divine and Its Relation to the Rational.* Translated by John W. Harvey. London: Oxford University Press, 1928.

Poirier, Richard. *A World Elsewhere: The Place of Style in American Literature.* London: Oxford University Press, 1966.

Richards, Grant. *Author Hunting by An Old Literary Sports Man.* New York: Coward McCann, Inc., 1934.

Ricoeur, Paul. *The Conflict of Interpretations: Essays in Hermeneutics.* Edited by Don Ihde. Evanston, Ill.: Northwestern University Press, 1974.

Rose, Anne C. *Transcendentalism as a Social Movement, 1830–1850.* New Haven: Yale University Press, 1981.

Ross-Bryant, Lynn. *Imagination and the Life of the Spirit: An Introduction to the Study of Religion and Literature.* Chico, Calif.: Scholars Press, 1981.

Smith, Henry Nash. *Virgin Land: The American West as Symbol and Myth.* Cambridge: Harvard University Press, 1950.

Spiller, R. E., ed. *Selected Essays, Lectures, and Poems of Ralph Waldo Emerson.* New York: Simon and Schuster, 1965.

Stegner, Wallace, ed. *The American Novel: From James Fenimore Cooper to William Faulkner.* New York: Basic Books, Inc., 1965.

Stewart, Randall. *American Literature and Christian Doctrine.* Baton Rouge: Louisiana State University Press, 1958.

Szasz, Ferenc Morton. *The Divided Mind of Protestant America, 1880–1930.* Tuscaloosa: The University of Alabama Press, 1982.

Tanner, Tony. *The Reign of Wonder: Naivety and Reality in American Literature.* Cambridge: The University Press, 1965.

van der Leeuw, G. *Religion in Essence and Manifestation: A Study in Phenomenology.* Translated by J. E. Turner. London: George Allen and Unwin, 1938.

Wagenknecht, Edward. *Cavalcade of the American Novel: From the Birth of the Nation to the Middle of the Twentieth Century.* New York: Holt, Rinehart and Winston, 1952.

Williams, Kenny J. *In the City of Men: Another Story of Chicago.* Nashville, Tenn.: Townsend Press, 1974.

————. *Prairie Voices: A Literary History of Chicago from the Frontier to 1893.* Nashville, Tenn.: Townsend Press, 1980.

Wilson, John F. *Public Religion in American Culture.* Philadelphia: Temple University Press, 1979.

Ziff, Larzer. *The American 1890s: Life and Times of a Lost Generation.* New York: The Viking Press, 1966.

Other Primary and Unpublished Sources

Eddins, John. "Systematic Theology Notes." Wake Forest, N.C.: Southeastern Baptist Theological Seminary. Spring 1981.

Emerson, Ralph Waldo. "Nature," "The Poet," "The American Scholar," "The Transcendentalist," and "Self-Reliance." All in *Selected Essays, Lectures, and Poems of Ralph Waldo Emerson,* edited by R. E. Spiller. New York: Simon and Schuster, 1965.

Kort, Wesley A. Durham, N.C.: Duke University. Conversations, 1985–1987.

Melville, Herman. *Moby Dick or the White Whale.* New York: New American Library, 1961. Originally published in 1851.

Thoreau, Henry David. *The Works of Thoreau,* edited by Henry Seidel Canby. Boston: Houghton Mifflin Company, 1937.

Wacker, Grant. "Introduction to the History of Religion in America Notes." Chapel Hill, the University of North Carolina at Chapel Hill. October 30, 1984.

Whitman, Walt. "Preface to the 1855 Edition of *Leaves of Grass,*" "Song of Myself," and "Crossing Brooklyn Ferry." All in *Leaves of Grass and Selected Prose,* edited by John Kouwenhoven. New York: The Modern Library, Random House, 1950.

Index